TOP
MONTREAL
AND QUEBEC CITY

Top 10 Montreal and Quebec City Highlights

The Top 10 of Everything

Welcome to Montreal
and Quebec City...........................5

Exploring Montreal
and Quebec City...........................6

Montreal and Quebec City
Highlights...................................10

Parc du Mont-Royal.....................12

Basilique Notre-Dame 16

Parc Olympique............................18

Pointe-à-Callière 22

Musée des Beaux-Arts
de Montréal 24

La Citadelle, Quebec City.............28

Musée de la Civilisation
de Québec...................................30

Basilique Sainte-Anne-
de-Beaupré..................................32

Île d'Orléans 34

Les Laurentides...........................36

Moments in History 40

Cultural Québécois 42

Historic Sites 44

Parks and Waterways..................46

Outdoor Activities.......................48

Children's Attractions 50

Performing Arts Venues..............52

Montreal and Quebec City
for Free......................................54

Festivals and Events 56

CONTENTS

Montreal and Quebec City Area by Area

Streetsmart

Vieux-Montréal
  and Vieux-Port..........................**60**

Downtown and Quartier Latin.....**68**

Mont-Royal to
  Hochelaga-Maisonneuve.........**78**

Excursions from Montreal..........**84**

Quebec City **92**

Getting Around **106**

Practical Information.................**108**

Places to Stay.............................**112**

General Index **118**

Acknowledgments **124**

Phrase Book................................**126**

Within each Top 10 list in this book, no hierarchy of quality or popularity is implied. All 10 are, in the editor's opinion, of roughly equal merit.

Throughout this book, floors are referred to in accordance with American usage; i.e., the "first floor" is at ground level.

Title page, front cover and spine *Beautiful skyline of Quebec City*
Back cover, clockwise from top left *Vieux Quebec by the Saint Lawrence River; Foliage at Lac-Superieur, Laurentides; Mont-Tremblant Ski Resort; Historic Quebec City; Saint Joseph Oratory*

The rapid rate at which the world is changing is constantly keeping the DK Eyewitness team on our toes. While we've worked hard to ensure that this edition of Montreal and Quebec City is accurate and up-to-date, we know that opening hours alter, standards shift, prices fluctuate, places close and new ones pop up in their stead. So, if you notice we've got something wrong or left something out, we want to hear about it. Please get in touch at **travelguides@dk.com**

Welcome to
Montreal and Quebec City

Montreal is often called the cultural capital of Canada. Spend a few days here, exploring its charming cobblestone streets and innovative museums, and it soon becomes evident why. Quebec City dates back to the early 17th century and is similarly rich in art and history. With DK Eyewitness Top 10 Montreal and Quebec City, it's yours to explore.

Montreal's Francophone roots have seeped into all aspects of life, from French-inspired cuisine to the theater scene. Wandering the cobblestone streets of **Vieux-Montréal** feels little different to strolling through the Marais in Paris. But Montreal is much more than its history: in one day, you'll gaze up at mirrored skyscrapers, sip espresso at a buzzy café, and top off the night at a rooftop club. The **Musée des Beaux-Arts** and year-round festivals, such as **Just for Laughs** and **Montreal Jazz Festival**, cement the city as a bastion of Canadian culture.

But you haven't truly experienced Quebec until you've visited Quebec City, which is North America's oldest surviving walled city. Walk the ancient turrets of Vieux-Québec, snap photos of the **Château Frontenac** and soak up local history in the **Musée de la Civilisation de Québec**. In the evening, catch a show at **Grand Théâtre de Québec**, and sample fresh produce at **Île d'Orleans**, known as the "Garden of Quebec."

Whether you're coming for a weekend or a week, our Top 10 guide is designed to bring together the best of everything these two cities have to offer. The guide gives you insider tips throughout, from free events and activities to the lowdown on hotels, plus easy-to-follow itineraries that tie together a slew of sights in a short space of time. Add inspiring photography and detailed maps, and you've got the essential pocket-sized travel companion. **Enjoy the book, and enjoy Montreal and Quebec City**.

Clockwise from top: **Stade Olympique, Montreal, Oratoire St-Joseph in Montreal, Marché Bonsecours in Montreal, Parc National du Mont-Tremblant, Outdoor seating in Old Town, Vieux-Port in Montreal, Ice-skaters in Quebec**

Exploring Montreal and Quebec City

Montreal and Quebec City abound in cultural riches, from art-packed museums, historic cathedrals, and theater to festivals, parks and waterfronts. Whether here for a weekend or a week, these two- and four-day itineraries will maximize your time.

Montreal's **botanical gardens** are an oasis in the heart of the city.

Two Days in Montreal

Day ❶
MORNING

Explore at your own pace the fascinating **Pointe-à-Callière** (see pp22–3), which brings the history of Montreal to life. Afterwards, saunter along Montreal's **Vieux-Port** (see pp60–67) and breezy waterfront, taking in views of the St Lawrence River along the way.

AFTERNOON

Stroll the cobblestone streets of Vieux-Montréal to the **Basilique Notre-Dame** (see pp16–17), a Gothic Revival masterpiece that is now the symbol of the city. Time your visit with one of the choral concerts that take place in the early evening.

Day ❷
MORNING

Peruse the **Musée des Beaux-Arts de Montréal** (see pp24–5), the oldest museum in the country, which traces the artistic timeline of Canada, from antiquities to contemporary works.

AFTERNOON

Head to the **Parc Olympique** (see pp18–21) and explore the complex, and then visit the fragrant **Jardin Botanique** (see pp20–21). Afterwards, tour Montreal's geographic gem: the forested slopes of **Parc du Mont-Royal** (see pp12–15). Walk a mountain trail leading to scenic lookouts, and watch the sun set over the skyline, with the river glinting in the distance.

Four Days in Montreal and Quebec City

Day ❶

MORNING
Start the morning in the heart of Vieux-Montréal: enjoy an espresso at a café, and then walk the narrow, historic streets to the **Basilique Notre-Dame** (see pp16–17).

AFTERNOON
Head down to the waterfront along the banks of the St Lawrence River, to the **Pointe-à-Callière** (see pp22–3), where you can learn more about Montreal's history.

Day ❷

MORNING
Kick off the day at the **Musée des Beaux-Arts de Montréal** (see pp24–5), Montreal's most celebrated museum. Then roam the leafy pathways of **Parc du Mont-Royal** (see pp12–15).

AFTERNOON
Take an afternoon getaway to **Les Laurentides** (see pp36–7): visit Val-David, a lively town with art galleries, restaurants, and mountain views.

Day ❸

MORNING
Head to Quebec City and start your explorations at the **Musée de la Civilisation de Québec** (see pp30–31), which covers centuries of history.

AFTERNOON
Stroll the beautifully preserved alleyways of Vieux-Québec, and then

The Musée de la Civilisation de Québec explores the region's history.

visit the elegant **Basilique Sainte-Anne-de-Beaupré** (see pp32–3), one of the oldest pilgrimage sites in North America.

Day ❹

MORNING
Explore the vast **La Citadelle** (see pp28–9), a military fortification that sprawls over 37 acres (15 ha). Visit for the Changing of the Guard (10am daily Jun–Sep). Bring a picnic lunch to enjoy on the verdant grounds.

AFTERNOON
Head to the charming **Île d'Orleans** (see pp34–5), stopping to view the thundering Montmorency Falls along the way. Walk or cycle around the island, visiting vineyards, restaurants, and artisan workshops to get a glimpse into historic Quebec.

Key
━━ Four-day itinerary

Top 10 Montreal and Quebec City Highlights

Changing of the Guard at La Citadelle, Quebec City, with Château Frontenac in the background

Montreal and Quebec City Highlights	10
Parc du Mont-Royal	12
Basilique Notre-Dame	16
Parc Olympique	18
Pointe-à-Callière	22
Musée des Beaux-Arts de Montréal	24

La Citadelle, Quebec City	28
Musée de la Civilisation de Québec	30
Basilique Sainte-Anne-de-Beaupré	32
Île d'Orléans	34
Les Laurentides	36

TOP10 Montreal and Quebec City Highlights

These two cities captivate with their history, culture, and festivity. Both major players in Canada's story, their portside locations have kept them at the heart of commerce, resulting in a charming blend of heritage architecture and modern venues.

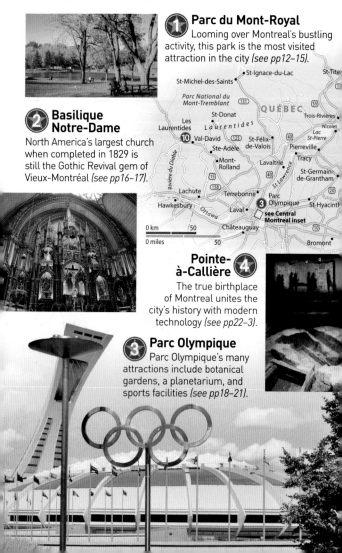

1 Parc du Mont-Royal
Looming over Montreal's bustling activity, this park is the most visited attraction in the city (see pp12–15).

2 Basilique Notre-Dame
North America's largest church when completed in 1829 is still the Gothic Revival gem of Vieux-Montréal (see pp16–17).

4 Pointe-à-Callière
The true birthplace of Montreal unites the city's history with modern technology (see pp22–3).

3 Parc Olympique
Parc Olympique's many attractions include botanical gardens, a planetarium, and sports facilities (see pp18–21).

Central Montreal

Parc du Mont-Royal ❶

Musée des Beaux-Arts de Montréal ❺

Basilique Notre-Dame ❷

Pointe-à-Callière ❹

QUARTIER LATIN

CHINATOWN

DOWNTOWN

VIEUX-MONTRÉAL

VIEUX-PORT

AV DES PINS OUEST

RUE SHERBROOKE OUEST

RUE SHERBROOKE EST

R STE-CATHERINE O

0 meters 1000
0 yards 1000

Basilique Sainte-Anne-de-Beaupré ❽

Île d'Orléans ❾

St-Raymond

Quebec City ❻ ❼

...rtneuf (40)

Donnacona

...t Lawrence

St-Agapit

Ste-Marie

(132)

(20)

(116)

...aveluyville

East Broughton

Plessisville

Warwick

Richmond

(55)

...erbrooke

❺ Musée des Beaux-Arts de Montréal

The largest in Quebec, this museum has works dating from antiquity to contemporary masters *(see pp24–5)*.

❻ La Citadelle, Quebec City

Three centuries of military presence continue in this working army base, home to Canada's first observatory *(see pp28–9)*.

❼ Musée de la Civilisation de Québec

Exhibits include artifacts from Indigenous peoples, Chinese *objets d'art*, and items from everyday life in Quebec *(see pp30–31)*.

Basilique Sainte-Anne-de-Beaupré ❽

Featuring 240 stained-glass windows and a gleaming mosaic, this granite basilica was built in 1923–63 *(see pp32–3)*.

❾ Île d'Orléans

This island of farm communities preserves the traditions of the original settlers *(see pp34–5)*.

Les Laurentides ❿

Visit the mountain range that has long been the favorite year-round playground for weekenders and vacationers with its pristine lakes, hiking trails, and ski slopes *(see pp36–7)*.

🔟 ⭐ Parc du Mont-Royal

The geographic highlight of Montreal is Mont-Royal's steep slopes. Named by Jacques Cartier in 1535, the protected district of Parc du Mont-Royal covers a large expanse of forested mountain, providing abundant green spaces, shrubs, and flowers, as well as habitats for hundreds of species of birds and other wildlife. Designed in 1876 by Frederick Law Olmsted, Mont-Royal still inspires locals as an arboreal delight in the center of their metropolis – activity options include skating, cycling, paddle-boating, tobogganing, and snowshoeing. To the northwest is the Oratoire St-Joseph.

Oratoire St-Joseph ①
The dome atop this shrine is an overwhelming sight to the west of the park **(right)**. Pilgrims flock to the oratory, inspired by tales of miracle cures *(see pp14–15)*.

② Lookouts
Belvedere Kondiaronk **(below)** is the lookout of the Chalet du Mont-Royal. The Camillien-Houde lookout faces east over the river. Locals often refer to it as "Lovers' Lookout."

③ Trail Systems
The park has a network of forested corridors, popular with cyclists and runners in summer and cross-country skiiers in winter.

⑤ La Croix
Standing 100 ft (31 m) high, the original steel cross **(right)** was erected by Paul de Chomedey, Sieur de Maisonneuve, in 1643.

④ Cemeteries
Cimetière Notre-Dame-des-Neiges (Catholic) and Cimetière Mont-Royal (non-Catholic) are the two main resting places of the city. Far from sombre, they are adorned with lovely statues, sculptures, and luxuriant plantings.

Map of Parc du Mont-Royal

1.5 km (1 mile)

CHEMIN DE LA CÔTE-DES-NEIGES

CHEMIN

Cimetière Mont-Royal

REMEMBRANCE

VOIE CAMILLIEN-HOUDE

AVE DU PARC

Parc   du   Mont-Royal

AVENUE   CEDAR

AVE DES PINS OUEST

FREDERICK LAW OLMSTED

A champion of the City Beautiful movement of landscape architects, Frederick Law Olmsted was born in Hartford, Connecticut in 1822. Best known for his visionary designs of Central Park in New York City, Olmsted's aim was to reject the formal plantations that had previously been in vogue and to complement the natural landscape with his pastoral designs and with designated areas for recreation.

6 Police Stables
Visits to the Police Cavalry Stables are possible, and it is common to see officers on horseback cantering through the park.

7 Maison Smith
Built for Boston merchant Hosea B. Smith in 1858, Maison Smith is home to Les Amis de la Montagne exhibitions, and is an entry point to the park.

8 Les Amis de la Montagne
This is the base of a citizen group focusing on the preservation of and education about both the historic and natural legacy of the park.

9 Lac aux Castors
The heart of Parc du Mont-Royal is Lac aux Castors. People gather during fair weather to paddle boats or to ice-skate in winter **(above)**.

10 Tam-Tam Festival
Sundays in the park during the summer belong to the exuberant Tam-Tam Festival. For decades, drummers, musicians, dancers, and artisans have spontaneously gathered around the Monument Sir George-Étienne Cartier where they party until dusk.

NEED TO KNOW
MAP C2 ■ (514) 843 8240
■ www.lemontroyal.qc.ca

Oratoire St-Joseph:
3800 Chemin Queen-Mary; (514) 733 8211; Mass: 8:30am, 10am, 11:30am, 2pm, 4:30pm & 7:30pm Mon–Sat, 8:30am, 9:30am, 11am, 1:30pm, 4:30pm & 7:30pm Sun; www.saint-joseph.org

■ If you are visiting Montreal in winter, take a snowshoe excursion through the park at night to enjoy the city lights.

■ Parking fees are high in Parc du Mont-Royal. Park inside the grounds of one of the cemeteries and walk to the lookout.

Features of Oratoire St-Joseph

1 Saint Brother André
Alfred Bessette, born in 1845, joined the Congregation of the Holy Cross in 1870. Here, as a humble cleric, he assumed the name of Brother André and began working extraordinary curative powers on the sick. He attributed his skills to St Joseph and petitioned for donations to build the Oratoire. He was canonized by Pope Benedict XVI in 2010.

2 Neo-Classical Architecture
Inspired by the temples of Corinth, architects Dalbé Viau and Alphonse Venne designed the exterior of St Joseph's, but the completion was a collaboration of Lucien Parent, monk Dom Paul Bellot, and architect Gérard Notebaert.

3 Saint Brother André's Tomb
Brother André died on January 6, 1937, at the age of 91. While his remains are buried in the church, his heart was removed and placed in a reliquary, and is still a popular draw for pilgrims. A beautiful fresco, created by Henri Charlier, decorates his tomb wall.

Pilgrims ascending the 99 Steps

4 99 Steps
There are 283 concrete steps leading from the street up to the crypt church, with 99 wooden steps in between. Dedicated pilgrims can be often seen struggling up the wooden steps on their knees.

5 Musée de l'Oratoire
An extensive religious art collection heads the permanent features on display in the Oratory Museum. The museum is also known for its large and unusual collection of nativity displays.

6 Crypt Church
Created in 1917 at the base of the basilica, the concrete structure of the crypt church is built into the mountainside and forms part of the Oratory's foundations. It has a main altar of Carrara marble and a 1,000-seat capacity. Don't miss the stunning stained-glass windows.

7 John XXIII Pavilion
A convenient overnight hostel adjacent to the parking area contains a souvenir shop and cafeteria. A resident organization also helps arrange personalized religious journeys for the faithful.

Saint Brother Andre's Tomb

THE HISTORY OF THE ORATOIRE ST-JOSEPH

The saga of Montreal's mammoth Oratoire St-Joseph began with the construction of a tiny chapel in 1904 by Brother André and friends. The final structural elements only came together in 1967 – 30 years after Brother André's death. More than 500 ft (150 m) above street level, it is a staggering 195 ft (60 m) from the floor to the peak of the dome – one of the largest in the world. Reminiscent of Italian Renaissance architecture, the basilica features Corinthian columns, stained-glass master-pieces, and a huge carillon (56 bells). More than two million visitors pack the monument each

Oratoire St-Joseph facade

year, with crutches and wheelchairs left behind as evidence of the cures taking place here. Brother André's followers had long been asking for his canonization. In accordance with the Catholic church, two posthumous miracles are needed to earn sainthood. The first, the cure of a cancer victim in 1958, led to his beatification in 1982. The second was in 1999, when a boy emerged from a coma after an accident. It made Brother André the 11th Canadian, and first Quebec-born, saint.

Canes hanging in the Votive Chapel

8 Votive Chapel

Canes, crutches, and other medical aids left behind by cured pilgrims line the walls in this small but inspirational chapel. Visitors can light a devotional candle, then walk past a statue of St Joseph to the room of Saint Brother André's tomb.

9 Altar and Stations of the Cross

The magnificent altar, crucifix, and wooden statues of the 12 Apostles are creations of the French artist Henri Charlier. Roger Villiers sculpted the Way of the Cross between 1957 and 1959, and the stunning interior mosaic was added to the altar in 1960.

10 Les Petits Chanteurs du Mont-Royal

Begun in 1956 by the then head of the church Father Brault, the oratory's choir is made up of 210 boys aged between 8 and 17. Their silky vocals embellish more than 70 religious festivities each year, at the oratory, around the country, and abroad. Their repertoire ranges from Georgian chant to modern choral works. The boys are schooled here when they are not performing.

TOP 10 ★ Basilique Notre-Dame

The most magnificent landmark of Vieux-Montréal is this huge Gothic Revival undertaking designed by Irish architect James O'Donnell and built between 1824 and 1829. This thriving Catholic church has a stunning medieval-style interior that features walnut wood carvings, exquisite stained-glass windows, 24-carat gold stars in a vaulted blue ceiling, plus one of the largest Casavant organs in North America. Don't miss the fine art paintings in the nave and the impressive Chapelle du Sacré-Coeur hidden behind the altar.

1 Gothic Revival Architecture
Rectangular in shape, contrary to the norms of the day, Notre-Dame features arcades with cross-ribbed vaulting.

2 Le Gros Bourdon
It is possible to hear the amazing chimes of Le Gros Bourdon, the largest bell in North America, 18 miles (30 km) outside Montreal.

3 The Altar
In 1880 local artists Henri Bouriché and Victor Bourgeau created complementary wood sculptures backed by azure for this amazing altarpiece **(right)**.

4 Chapelle du Sacré-Coeur
Opened in 1891, this delightful gem **(left)** is concealed behind the main altar. Countless marriage ceremonies take place here, inspiring the moniker, "The Wedding Chapel."

NEED TO KNOW

MAP K3 ■ 110 Rue Notre-Dame Ouest, Place d'Armes ■ (514) 842 2925 ■ www. basiliquenotredame.ca

Open 8am–4:30pm Mon–Fri, 8am–4pm Sat, 12:30–4pm Sun
Adm $6

■ **Maison Christian Faure** *(355 Place Royale)* serves delicate and delicious pastries as well as sweets and sandwiches.

■ Breathtaking sound and light *(son et lumière)* shows, called AURA, are held daily.

JAMES O'DONNELL

Irish architect James O'Donnell was contracted to draw plans and oversee the construction of Basilique Notre-Dame in 1823. A Protestant by birth, O'Donnell's pride in the basilica caused him to convert to Catholicism, allowing him burial inside "his" church. Synthesizing many divergent design elements from contributing architects, he introduced the Gothic Revival style into Canadian architecture.

7 Stained-Glass Windows

In 1929 Olivier Maurault, a priest and author, conceived the present-day windows **(above)**, which depict early religious events and scenes from the lives of the people of Vieux-Montréal.

Plan of Basilique Notre-Dame

8 Daudelin Sculpture

The sculptor Charles Daudelin's bronze *reredos* **(above)**, which hangs behind the Chapelle du Sacré-Coeur, is among his most dramatic works.

5 The Pulpit

Architect Victor Bourgeau's first known work is the 1844 spiral staircase pulpit, resembling tiers of a wedding cake. Set in the middle of the church, it allows sermons to be heard without amplification.

9 Famous Weddings

Many famous couples have tied the knot in Notre-Dame, but the best-known celebrity wedding is that of singer Céline Dion in 1994 *(see p43)*.

6 Séminaire St-Sulpice

Built in 1685 by the Sulpician order, this stone structure standing beside the basilica is the second oldest building in Montreal *(see p61)*.

10 Casavant Organ

Blacksmith Joseph Casavant was the first significant builder of pipe organs in Canada. He built the Notre-Dame organ **(right)** for the basilica in 1891.

🔟 ⭐ Parc Olympique

One of Montreal's most remarkable attractions, Parc Olympique is also one of its most controversial. Built for the 1976 Olympic Games, it remained unfinished until the 1980s, and the retractable roof over the stadium has never fully worked. Nevertheless, visitors can easily spend a full day or two entertained by the varied exhibitions, sights, and activities within this immense quadrilateral. Ride the funicular to the top of the Tour Montréal for the most enthralling view of the region.

Stade Olympique ①
Designed by the French architect Roger Taillibert and constructed by local engineers for the 1976 Olympics, the stadium **(right)** seats 60,000 people, has a cable-suspended roof and is covered in a membrane of space-age Kevlar material. Today it is used to stage events such as rock concerts.

② Centre Sportif
This sports complex houses five swimming pools with continuously recirculating water. Other facilities include a fitness suite, yoga studios, a center for scuba diving, and a café.

④ Planétarium Rio Tinto Alcan
Opened in 2013, this fascinating museum **(right)** has state-of-the-art technology explaining everything from the building blocks of life on earth to the many wonders of the universe (see p51).

③ Aréna Maurice-Richard
Named after the Montreal Canadiens hockey legend Maurice "Rocket" Richard **(right)**, the indoor rink continues to promote the sport. The museum "Univers Maurice-Richard" features the scoring ace's memorabilia.

⑤ Tour Montréal
For great views ride the extraordinary funicular in the Tour Montréal. An observatory sits atop the world's highest leaning tower, almost 541 ft (165 m) from ground to summit.

⑥ Marché Maisonneuve
More than just a taste of fresh market fare, the Marché Maisonneuve attracts clientele from all over the province, and is the perfect spot for people-watching.

Map of Parc Olympique

MAYOR JEAN DRAPEAU

Many agree that the enthusiasm of Jean Drapeau, the mayor of Montreal from 1954 to 1957 and again from 1960 to 1986, put Montreal on the international map. A lawyer by trade, he was passionate about his city, and while in office oversaw the building of the Métro subway system and the city's cultural venue Place des Arts, brought the World's Fair to town in 1967, and was largely responsible for the successful bid for the 1976 Olympic Games.

NEED TO KNOW

MAP P6 ■ 4545 Rue Pierre-de-Coubertin ■ Métro Pie-IX ■ (514) 252 4141 ■ www.parcolympique.qc.ca

Adm to specific attractions

Jardin Botanique: 4101 Rue Sherbrooke Est; (514) 868 3000; open mid-May–Oct: 9am–6pm daily, Nov–mid-May: 9am–5pm daily, closed Mon in Nov–May; adm; www.espacepourlavie.ca

■ The best place to eat, for both price and atmosphere, is Café Olimpico in the Mile End district (see p82).

■ The "Since 1976" is a permanent and free exhibit in the Tour Montréal featuring artifacts, photos, and digital content about the history of the Parc Olympique.

7 Insectarium

Quebecer Georges Brossard, also known as "the Bug Man," roams the world collecting exotic insects, and then displays them in this riveting showcase *(see p50)*.

8 Jardin Botanique

Founded in 1931 and covering nearly 185 acres (75 ha), the lush gardens were created by gifted horticulturist Henry Teuscher *(see pp20–21)*.

9 Biodôme

Home to ecological attractions, with local plants, animals, and birds of the tropical forest. The Biodôme reopened in 2020 after renovations *(see p50)*.

10 Musée Château Dufresne

The Gothic-inspired private residence **(below)** was originally designed and constructed by Parisian architect Jules Rénard for Oscar and Marius Dufresne from 1915 to 1918. It now welcomes a variety of decorative and informative exhibitions.

Jardin Botanique Features

Tranquil Lac de Rêve

Look out for the rainforest canopy, tropical medicinal plants, and beautiful, brightly colored orchids.

(1) Lac de Rêve
A lush domain, Lac de Rêve is located at the center of the Chinese Gardens. Visitors can watch resident geese and ducks, relax in a comfortable area, or wander through the landscaped lake area surrounded by rock gardens and bridges.

(2) First Nations Garden
This 6-acre (2.5-ha) garden highlights the deep bond the First Nations and Inuit have with plants and nature. The garden features several interactive terminals, shows, and special events. The area is divided up into five different zones: hardwood and softwood forests, an exploration of Nordic life, an interpretation pavilion, and a gathering area.

(3) Greenhouses
A series of greenhouses in the gardens, just past the entrance, provide enough humidity for various botanical environments to thrive.

(4) Sukiya Japanese Tea Pavilion
Honoring the traditional Japanese home, architect Hisato Hiraoka has gathered together the artistic ideals of Japanese society within this graceful structure. There is an art gallery, Zen and bonsai gardens, and an exhibition room.

(5) Chinese Gardens
These traditionally designed Chinese gardens are one of the largest outside China, and are home to seven classical structures inspired by the Ming Dynasty.

Lovingly nurtured Chinese Gardens

(6) Wu Yee-Sun Bonsai Collection
At any time of year, the captivating Wu Yee-Sun Collection of miniature bonsai trees is on permanent exhibit inside their greenhouse. This is one of the most impressive and largest collections of its kind in the world.

(7) Frédéric Back Tree Pavilion
Situated in the northeast sector of the gardens, this interpretation center and interactive exhibition is laid out in four parts: Trees in our History, Anatomy and Growth, Trees and the Forest, and The Many Uses of Trees.

One of several greenhouses

8 Mini train

Since the gardens are spread out over many acres, it's a good idea to take advantage of the popular mini train, which circulates continuously throughout the day along the paved pathways. Clearly marked areas within the gardens indicate where the bright red trains make regular stops for boarding or disembarking.

A mini train in the gardens

9 Libraries

There are two fascinating libraries situated within the gardens. The public library features an extensive children's section. There is also an academic library that is home to numerous scientific books, journals, and papers, including studies of botany.

10 Children's Highlights

Exciting and informative features in the garden are part of the ongoing effort to educate Montreal children and bring them closer to nature. Exhibitions that would interest kids include the Youth Gardens, Butterflies Go Free, the BuzzGround Playground, and the Insectarium *(see p50)*.

HISTORY OF THE JARDIN BOTANIQUE

In 1931, Montreal's mayor, Camillien Houde, conceived a master plan to put the unemployed to work by building the city's first botanical gardens. He hired architect Lucien Keroack to design the main building, and work began in the midst of a deep economic depression. Owing much to the Christian Brothers religious sect and particularly to Brother Marie-Victorin for his visionary concept, the team invited American landscape architect and botanist Henry Teuscher to establish the permanent collections and design the site. By 1938 the greenhouses were built and Montreal has enjoyed this rich horticultural domain ever since.

TOP 10
FLORA IN THE JARDIN BOTANIQUE

1 Aroids
2 Begonias
3 Bonsai and penjing
4 Ferns
5 Bromeliads
6 Cactuses and succulents
7 Cyads
8 Orchids
9 Lilacs and lotus
10 Gesneriads

The Jardin Botanique features an impressive collection of bonsai trees.

🌟 Pointe-à-Callière

Ascending like a sentinel from the confluence of the St Pierre and St Lawrence rivers, this National Historic Site honors the founding of Montreal at Place Royale. Within this landmark of stone and brushed steel are three sections: a chic building constructed on top of the ruins of older structures; the archaeological crypt; and the renovated Customs House. A self-guided tour system allows each visitor to explore at their own pace, but guides throughout the site will answer questions and bring the history of the city to life.

1 Éperon Building

Architect Dan S. Hanganu designed this edifice to create a building that is an exhibition in itself. The front door marks the spot of the first shelter in Ville-Marie (1642).

2 Tales of a City

This 18-minute voyage through the history of Montreal is an inspired introduction to the museum, enchanting visitors and setting the stage for a memorable visit.

3 First Catholic Cemetery in North America

Residents from the earliest days of the original fortification created a cemetery under Place Royale. When the museum excavated the site, the discovery resulted in this exhibit (**below**).

The vast Pointe-à-Callière site

4 Where Montreal Began

This exhibition (**above**) houses fascinating artifacts that represent more than 600 years of local history, from precontact times to the present day.

5 Underground Vaulted Conduit

Montreal's earliest sewer and plumbing system, dating from the 18th century, can be seen in this network of conduits, beneath a cobblestoned walkway. Another excavation revealed the St Pierre River.

**Plan of
Pointe-à-Callière**

Key to Floorplan

- Basement
- Ground floor
- First floor
- Second floor
- Third floor
- Fourth floor

HISTORY OF
THE MUSEUM

In 1642 Paul de Chomedey, Sieur de Maisonneuve, founded the settlement of Ville-Marie, now Montreal, on this site. More than 350 years later, a series of excavations unearthed over one million artifacts that painted a picture of the daily life of New France's earliest settlers. Pointe-à-Callière opened here to display these artifacts. A permanent archaeological dig is now in place in the area.

8 Models At Your Feet

Virtual technology bridges past and present here. Meet historic figures, hear archaeological explanations, and view five centuries of artifacts under glass beneath your feet.

NEED TO KNOW

MAP K3 ▪ 350 Place Royale at Rue de la Commune ▪ (514) 872 9150 ▪ www.pac musee.qc.ca

Open 10am–5pm Tue–Fri, 11am–5pm Sat & Sun

Adm $25 adults; $24 senior citizens; $17 students (13–17); $8 children; under-5s free

▪ One of the best views in all of Vieux-Montréal is available from L'Arrivage Bistro, on the top level of the museum. It serves great French cuisine, and has a reasonably priced table d'hôte menu at lunch.

6 Market Day, 1750

This interactive fresco is set in the remains of the main gate that led to the marketplace in 1750. Visitors can see virtual figures and play out scenes from their lives.

9 A Customs House and its Architect

Montreal's old Customs House, built between 1836 and 1837, is a Neo-Classical building designed by John Ostell. It has been carefully renovated to its original state and houses a permanent exhibition.

10 Montreal Love Stories

This series of intimate portraits draws on photographs, videos, and first-hand accounts of Montrealers.

7 Youville Pumping Station Interpretation Center

Across from the museum an old pumping station **(above)** has exhibits on science and technology.

🔟 ⭐ Musée des Beaux-Arts de Montréal

One of the most impressive museums in North America dominates both sides of Rue Sherbrooke Ouest. It began life in 1860, when a group of collectors set up the Art Association of Montreal to present exhibitions, establish an art school, assemble a permanent collection of paintings, and develop an art library. They eventually constructed the Michal and Renata Hornstein Pavilion to house Old Masters and contemporary works. In 1991, the museum expanded into the Jean-Noël Desmarais Pavilion.

① Venice, Looking out over the Lagoon

A voyeur of the human landscape, Morrice is known for his departure from centuries of art tradition and for his philosophy of painting for painting's sake, seen in this work.

② Portrait of the Lawyer Hugo Simons

Otto Dix's artistic freedom is evident in this 1929 portrait of lawyer Hugo Simons. The image, bathed in reddish-copper tones, shows Dix's wish to portray his subjects' souls in his works.

③ Apelles Painting the Portrait of Campaspe

Italian artist Tiepolo uses the unusual technique of a painting-within-a-painting in this 1726 work **(above)**. Notice the artwork hanging on the wall of the studio, one of Tiepolo's own, entitled *The Bronze Serpent*.

④ Octobre

An example of James Tissot's control and mastery of space, this 1877 allegorical work is of his muse and mistress Kathleen Irene Newton **(left)**.

⑤ Judith with the Head of Holofernes, Dido

In these two paintings (1500), Andrea Mantegna demonstrates typical Renaissance traits: absence of emotion, knowledge of anatomy, and determinism of line.

⑥ Portrait of a Young Woman

A combined use of light, color, texture, and setting brings a feeling of intimacy to this **(above)** 1665 Rembrandt work.

The Tribute Money
10 Philippe de Champaigne's 1655 work portrays the Biblical tale of the Pharisees in this dramatic religious painting. The figure on the right is said to be a self-portrait **(left)**.

Plan of Musée des Beaux-Arts de Montréal

The Wheel
7 Montreal's best-known contemporary painter, Jean-Paul Riopelle, lets his spatula work its magic on this canvas (1954–5), creating a mosaic of elements, colors, and tones.

Key to Floorplan
- Level 4
- Level 3
- Level S2

The Black Star
8 Paul-Émile Borduas attended the École des Beaux-Arts in Montreal. This 1957 painting won a posthumous Guggenheim award in 1960 as the best Canadian painting in a New York gallery; the work has now returned to the artist's home town.

Mauve Twilight
9 Painted in 1921, this work is an evocative impression of winter by one of Quebec's most loved artists, Ozias Leduc. His ability to capture the light of dusk here confirms his talent for perfectly representing the provincial landscape.

5 Judith with the Head of Holofernes, Dido

The Tribute Money **10**

Octobre **4**

6 Portrait of a Young Woman

Venice, Looking out over the Lagoon **1**

3 Apelles Painting the Portrait of Campaspe

2 Portrait of the Lawyer Hugo Simons

8 The Black Star

7 The Wheel

Mauve Twilight **9**

NEED TO KNOW

MAP C3 ■ (514) 285 2000 ■ 1339–80 Rue Sherbrooke Ouest ■ www.mbam.qc.ca

Open 10am–5pm Thu–Sun, 10am–9pm Wed

■ On-site Le Beaux-Arts restaurant serves delicious but expensive French bistro cuisine (see p74), but there is also the inexpensive Petit Café in the same area of the Jean-Noël Desmarais Pavilion.

Museum Guide
There are five pavilions that make up the museum; the Michal and Renata Hornstein Pavilion (world cultures), which contains the Liliane and David M. Stewart Pavilion featuring decorative arts. The Jean-Noël Desmarais Pavilion, connected via a tunnel from Level S2, features international art. The Claire and Marc Bourgie Pavilion features Canadian and Quebec art, and the Michal and Renata Hornstein Pavilion for Peace is devoted to the world's artistic heritage.

Following pages Lac de Rêve, Jardin Botanique, Montreal

TOP 10 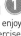 La Citadelle, Quebec City

Set atop Cap Diamant, this installation of 24 buildings is the largest military fortification in North America. Overlooking the St Lawrence River, the site was begun by the French in 1693, but much of the star-shaped battlement seen today was constructed by the British between 1820 and 1850, built to defend the city from possible invasion from the United States in the 19th century. The fort is home to the Royal 22nd Regiment of the Canadian Armed Forces and daily military spectacles are staged for visitors during the summer.

Changing of the Guard ①
One of the most enjoyable military exercises (right) involves precision marching with a musical escort. It is headed by Batisse the goat, the regiment's mascot.

② Dalhousie Gate
Named in honor of 13th-century Castle Dalhousie in Scotland, this formal entrance provides general access to La Citadelle and is the point at which processions and parades enter the grounds (above).

③ Fortifications
The impressive fortress (right) contains all of the most important elements for a strong military installation: height over the enemy, 360-degree visibility, difficult access, and durability. Although it has all of this to its advantage, La Citadelle has never, in fact, been attacked by an enemy.

④ Outer Walls
In 1820, under the British Lieutenant-Colonel Elias Walker Durnford, building of the outer walls of the polygon structure began. No one could access the Great Lakes or the Atlantic Ocean without coming under the watchful eye of La Citadelle's forces.

⑤ Museums
The collections unveiled in the two museums located here include everyday items used by soldiers over the centuries, a collection of rare military documents, ceremonial uniforms, antique armaments, precious art, and many other eclectic items.

Plan of La Citadelle

8 Redoubt
Tucked away into sections of the fieldstone walls, cannons protect their flanks without the need for backup support.

9 Firing of the Cannon
The firing of the cannon is an exciting event that takes place at the Citadelle every day at noon. It's a fine illustration of the military might the fort once displayed.

6 Chapel
Since army life requires long periods of working far from home, efforts were made to include elements of daily life at the fortification, including a chapel.

7 Governor-General's Residence
Since 1872, the Governor General has resided in this 153-room home during the summer months.

10 Barracks
A large part of the site is given over to housing the troops. Tanks used in past battles by the regiment are also on display (above).

⬛10 ⭐ Musée de la Civilisation de Québec

Few museums in the world receive the kind of rave reviews given to the Musée de la Civilisation de Québec (MCQ). The exhibitions (two of which are permanent) cover history, culture, sports, science, and intellectual and esoteric themes in a range of interactive ways that entertain and educate visitors. Designed by the celebrated architect Moshe Safdie, creator of Ottawa's National Gallery, the MCQ's main building is only one of its sites. The museum also incorporates the Musée de l'Amérique Francophone and the Séminaire de Québec, to produce a vibrant look at local life in all its facets.

1 Séminaire de Québec

Three superb exhibitions in the seminary form the largest religious collection in North America. The artifacts document the early religious education of the city.

2 The Chapel of the Séminaire de Québec

Information about Catholic rites and church decoration can be found inside the chapel.

3 Musée de l'Amérique Francophone

Exhibitions include the colonial history of North America, Francophone culture in North America, and local arts and crafts.

Facade of the MCQ

4 Joseph the Boarder

An enchanting interactive presentation, located in the Jérôme-Demers Pavilion, recalls daily life in Le Petit Séminaire de Québec for "Joseph," a typical waif in the early days of Nouvelle-France.

People of Québec... 5 Then and Now

Visitors can relive 400 years of Quebec's history, meeting figures and admiring objects from yesterday **(right)** and connecting to a past that is still shaping the events of today.

NEED TO KNOW

MAP M4 ▪ 85 Rue Dalhousie, Basse-Ville, Quebec City ▪ (418) 643 2158 ▪ www.mcq.org

Musée de la Civilisation de Québec: open 10am–5pm Tue–Sun; mid-Jun–Labor Day: 10am–5pm daily

Musée de l'Amérique Francophone and Séminaire de Québec: Closed for renovations until 2024

Adm 65 and over $19, 35–64s $20, 18–34s $15, 12–17s $7, families $45, under-11s free

▪ The on-site Café 47, near the coat-check area, offers reasonably priced good food.

▪ For a more leisurely experience, visit only those parts that you are most interested in.

7 Encounter with First Nations

This magnificent exhibition of First Nations' treasures **(left)** has over 500 objects displayed covering the history of the Indigenous peoples.

8 Make Way for the Middle Ages

Based around the workings of a medieval French village, this costume workshop explores how certain aspects of life in the Middle Ages have influenced how we live in the modern age.

SEPARATISM

Ever since the British made an offer in 1848 to allow the French to maintain their language within an English-speaking domain, the relationship between what would become the nation of Canada and the province of Quebec has been fraught with mistrust. As Canada and Quebec repeatedly experienced political deadlock, separatist sentiment grew. Many Québécois feel that their province is distinct from the rest of Canada, and so would be better off as a separate nation. In 1980 and 1995, referendums were held on whether to separate, and both times the vote was a narrow "no."

9 Église Notre-Dame-des-Victoires

Originally built in 1687, this French colonial stone church is the city's oldest. It was mostly destroyed by British bombs in 1759 but has since been restored several times (see p94).

10 Ephemeral Art

In summer, Musée de la Civilisation's roof displays art installations, with a backdrop of the Old Port and the St Lawrence River.

Map of Museum Sites

6 Place-Royale

Life as it was in Nouvelle-France comes alive at Place-Royale **(right)**; historic events are held on the site of the first settlement.

TOP 10 ★ Basilique Sainte-Anne-de-Beaupré

One of the oldest pilgrimage sites in North America began life in 1658 as a shrine to this patron saint of Quebec and was established as a basilica in 1887. The present church, started in 1923 but completed in 1963, has a striking interior with sumptuous decoration. Medical aids stacked beside the medieval-style entrance are testimony to the healing powers associated with the basilica. Stunning religious statues frame the entrance and line the luxurious gardens.

1 Candlelight Processions

It is common to witness evening candlelight processions honoring saints and religious holidays; those on July 25 and 26 celebrate Ste Anne.

2 Stained-Glass Windows

Considered by some to be the most beautiful since the Middle Ages, these dazzling 240 stained-glass windows **(above)** depict moments in the life of Ste Anne. The centerpiece is a huge oval window flooding light into the nave.

The impressive nave

3 Medieval Architecture

A five-nave towered church **(left)** blends imposing Gothic architecture with Romanesque details previously unseen in Quebec Province.

4 Memorial Chapel

This votive chapel, built in 1878 to commemorate the original church on this site, contains religious memorabilia, rare documents, and artifacts.

NEED TO KNOW

MAP P3 ■ 10018 Ave Royale, Sainte-Anne-de-Beaupré ■ (418) 827 3781 ■ www.sanctuairesainte anne.org

Open daily

■ To get a wonderful view of the church complex and the river, take a 10-minute walk from the gardens down the Rue de la Sanctuaire toward the Île d'Orléans Channel to the Quai de la Paix. This is a great spot to take photos.

■ Call ahead to check the opening hours for specific sites or for information regarding any special celebrations or festivities taking place. The cathedral can be crowded on feast days and religous holidays.

Plan of Basilique Sainte-Anne-de-Beaupré

2 kms
(1.2 miles)

9 Way of the Cross Bronzes

Life-size statues line the hillside trail beside the basilica. Honoring saints and Apostles, these add a Renaissance feeling to the grounds **(below)**.

5 St Augustin

Thomas Baillairgé continued his family's legacy as a religious decorator by carving pieces for the basilica, including an impressive statue of St Augustin.

8 Scala Santa

A wonderful little chapel constructed in 1891 includes a remarkable stairway venerating the one Jesus ascended to face condemnation by Pontius Pilate.

10 Relics

Three notable relics are housed in the Basilica - partial finger bones and two sets of forearm bones, all supposedly from Sainte Anne.

6 Atelier Paré

This woodcarver's workshop is worth a visit to see the artisan at work creating pieces for the basilica.

Sainte Anne's Fountain 7

Erected in 2008, this beautiful fountain **(right)** comprises a 13-ft (4-m) bronze basin with a statue of Sainte Anne holding her daughter, Mary rising from the center.

Île d'Orléans

A haven of greenery and tranquility, Île d'Orléans was one of the first European settlements in the Americas. Ever since Jacques Cartier arrived here in 1535, the six parishes along this 18-mile (30-km) island have maintained many of the French traditions of the first settlers, and over 600 heritage buildings present a preserved architectural gem. Rich with fertile soil, the island produces an abundance of local food that draws thousands of visitors every year.

1 Île de Bacchus
When Jacques Cartier found wild grape vines here he named it Île de Bacchus after the Greek god of wine, then changed the name to honor the Duke of Orleans.

2 Domaine Steinbach
Domaine Steinbach, in St-Pierre, welcomes visitors for organic cider tastings, and also makes vinegar and mustards.

NEED TO KNOW

MAP P3 ■ Dufferin-Montmorency highway 440

Bureau d'information touristique:
490 côte du Pont, St-Pierre-de-l'Île-d'Orléans; (418) 828 9411; www.tourisme.iledorleans.com

■ **Auberge Restaurant Les Ancêtres in Saint-Pierre** *(1101 Chemin Royal; (418) 828 2718)* offers fine cuisine and rooms, each named after ancestors who once lived here.

■ The tranquility here makes it a perfect spot to rent a bicycle, follow the walking guide from the Interpretation Center, or enjoy a picnic beside the river.

The town of St-Jean on Île d'Orléans

3 Montmorency Falls
Higher than Niagara Falls, Montmorency Falls **(below)** are a dramatic sight before you cross the bridge onto the island *(see p102)*.

4 Auberge la Goéliche
Located in the lovely community of Ste-Pétronille, the Auberge la Goéliche offers guests old-world hospitality, food, and ambiance.

6 Manoir Mauvide-Genest

This 1734 manor **(left)** is one of the oldest buildings in the province and a fine example of rural architecture from the 18th century. There's a small on-site museum and a seasonal market.

7 Horatio Walker Studio

The Canadian landscape artist Horatio Walker was a resident of the island, and his studio has been preserved in Ste-Pétronille on the street renamed in his honor. His legacy continues in the work of other island painters such as Horace Champagne.

FÉLIX LECLERC

Île d'Orléans, and Quebec as a whole, will forever be entwined with the artistry of Félix Leclerc (1914–88), who lived on the island and wrote about it extensively. The legacy of this prolific singer, songwriter, poet, and playwright *(see p42)*, and his ability to perfectly express the Québécois sensibility is honored at L'Espace Félix-Leclerc *(1214 Chemin Royal, St-Pierre; open daily)* where there is a permanent exhibition on his work, as well as a library and a gift shop.

Map of Île d'Orléans

5 Chocolaterie de l'Île d'Orléans

Ste-Pétronille is home to the most wonderful chocolate-maker in the province **(below)**, who also sells delicious homemade ice cream, jellies, and other edible goodies. It houses an interpretation center that explains the process of creating chocolate.

8 Le Vignoble Ste-Pétronille

With an incredible view across the St Lawrence River to Montmorency Falls, this 60-acre vineyard **(right)** is an excellent example of a quality, cold-weather grape-bearing plantation that creates popular red, white, and rosé wines.

9 Bureau d'accueil Touristique

The island's friendly tourist office offers excellent maps, brochures, audio guides, and local advice on where to stay and what to do.

10 La Forge-à-Pique-Assaut

The forge offers a fascinating opportunity to look inside a blacksmith's workshop. See artisan Guy Bel at work, as he continues to labor here, admirably maintaining traditional metal-working techniques.

TOP 10 ⭐ Les Laurentides

Les Laurentides (the Laurentians) are part of a shield of forested peaks enclosed by the Ottawa, St Lawrence, and Saguenay rivers, and are known for their ski slopes, which roll into sight one hour north of Montreal. First Nations relics indicate that the area was first settled by Indigenous peoples over 4,000 years ago. Since the 19th century the region has been a rich agricultural zone and is famous for fishing in its 6,000 lakes and ponds. It also offers many other outdoor activities, with numerous cycling and hiking trails in summer, and luxury ski resorts in winter.

1 St-Sauveur-des-Monts
Downhill skiing is the draw here in winter, but in summer the artisans' shops, restaurants, and galleries tempt visitors to town **(below)**.

2 Mont-Rolland
The historic homes in this laid-back village were built to house workers of the Rolland Mill, which was once the main employer of this forested domain.

3 Ste-Adèle
Spectacular outdoor recreation within easy reach of Montreal attracted the first tourist train to Ste-Adèle in 1891, and the town continues to welcome ski enthusiasts to its challenging slopes today.

4 Ville d'Estérel
A lush, rolling area including Ste-Marguerite-du-Lac-Masson, the village where renowned artist Jean-Paul Riopelle painted for many years. The area was originally developed by a Belgian aristocrat in the 1930s.

5 Val-Morin
Located along the P'tit Train du Nord cycle path, this tiny Francophone village beguiles visitors as the trail meanders around Lac Raymond. Skiers can take to the slopes at the ski resort Belle Neige.

NEED TO KNOW

MAP N5

Maison de Tourisme de Laurentides: Port du Nord, Exit 51, Highway 15; (450) 224 7007; www.laurentides.com

■ Visit the busy La Table des Gourmets in Val-David for unpretentious yet sophisticated French food. The restaurant is run by Breton-born chef, Thierry Rouyé, and his wife, Pascale.

■ Reasonably priced and comfortable log cabins are available on a first-come-first-served basis inside the Parc National de Mont-Tremblant ((418) 890 6527).

6 St-Jovite
The gateway to the Mont-Tremblant commercial district, the village of St-Jovite **(left)** offers visitors boutiques and traditional Québécois restaurants. Visit the palatial Monastère des Apôtres de l'Amour Infini just east of town.

7 Ste-Agathe-des-Monts
With its fishing, swimming, and skiing, Ste-Agathe-des-Monts became the first resort in Les Laurentides over 100 years ago.

"JACKRABBIT" JOHANNSEN
Born in Norway in 1875, Herman "Jackrabbit" Johannsen settled in the Montreal area with his wife and children in 1928. First Nations residents apparently gave him his nickname after watching him moving mysteriously and swiftly across the snow. This remarkable man, who lived an active outdoor life until the age of 111, put the Laurentian Mountains on the global ski map and was responsible for bringing cross-country skiing to Canada.

9 Parc National du Mont-Tremblant
The second largest of an awe-inspiring list of provincial parks **(left)**, it provides a haven for black bears, white-tailed deer, moose, wolves, raccoons, and over 200 species of birds. Outdoor activities include canoeing, fishing, and cross-country skiing.

8 Val-David
An enthralling town peppered with art galleries, which hosts music and poetry festivals, and is known for its rock climbing culture.

Map of Les Laurentides

Lac-Clef
St-Donat-de-Montcalm
Mont Tremblant △ 900m
Mont Tremblant
a Conception
St-Faustin
St-Jovite
Ste-Marguerite-du-Lac-Masson
Ste-Agathe-des-Monts
Val-David
Val-Morin
Ste-Adèle
Mt-Rolland
St-Sauveur-des-Monts

10 Mont Tremblant
This **(above)** is the highest peak in Les Laurentides at over 900 m (2,950 ft) and one of the most popular ski resorts in North America. Spas, shops, excellent dining, and live entertainment all add to the appeal.

The Top 10
of Everything

The Neo-Classical Marché
Bonsecours, Montreal

Moments in History	**40**	Children's Attractions	**50**
Cultural Québécois	**42**	Performing Arts Venues	**52**
Historic Sites	**44**	Montreal and Quebec City for Free	**54**
Parks and Waterways	**46**		
Outdoor Activities	**48**	Festivals and Events	**56**

🔟 Moments in History

Iroquoian settlement on the shores of the St Lawrence River

1 First Nations

Iroquoian and nomadic Algonquian peoples have lived in Quebec for thousands of years. "Kebec" is an Algonquian word meaning "place where the river narrows." Precontact, this area was used for hunting, gathering, and trade.

2 Jacques Cartier

The French explorer Jacques Cartier followed Basque fishing routes up the St Lawrence River, claiming Canada for King François I of France in 1534. He continued up the river in 1535 to land at the First Nations village of Hochelaga. Here he had one of several meetings with the Indigenous peoples, some of whom guided him.

3 Samuel de Champlain

French settlement began in 1608 when Samuel de Champlain (1567–1635) arrived in the region. He pushed out the Indigenous peoples who were living on the site of Quebec City, forcing them to eventually settle in what we now know as Wendake.

4 British Takeover

The struggle between the French and British in Europe continued in the Americas. Eventually, in 1759 after a summer-long stand-off, British General James Wolfe won claim to the province during the less than 30-minute siege of Quebec City on the Plains of Abraham. However, in 1774 the French were granted language and religion rights (see p31).

5 The Creation of Canada

After the Constitutional Act (1791) separated the colony into Upper Canada (southern Ontario) and Lower Canada (southern Quebec), British Lord Durham was sent to solve the ongoing problems between the English and French halves. He declared the Union Act of 1841, which fused the two sides under a single English-speaking parliament and effectively marginalized the French. By 1848, the English were forced to accept the use of French in order to avoid a backlash. On July 1, 1867, Quebec and Ontario joined with Nova Scotia and New Brunswick to form the Dominion of Canada, a federated kingdom in its own right.

The siege of Quebec City, 1759

6 The Dark Years
Well into the 20th century the Roman Catholic church held considerable political sway in Quebec. Maurice Duplessis' right-wing Union Nationale (1936–9 and 1944–59) used the church's moral influence to gain votes and accepted $100-million-worth of graft.

7 The Quiet Revolution
The collusion of church and state led to widespread resentment among Québécois. With the death of Duplessis, liberal sentiment grew. In 1960, the Liberal Party was elected, leading to province-wide social reforms and economic development.

8 The October Crisis
Political deadlock with Canada increased support for the separatist movement among Québécois. In October 1970 the radical separatist Front de Libération du Québec (FLQ) kidnapped two high-ranking politicians, murdering one of them.

René Lévesque, ex-leader of the PQ

9 Parti Québécois
René Lévesque's separatist Parti Québécois (PQ) was in power from 1976 to 1985 and ensured French-language dominance in Quebec with Bill 101, alarming the province's Anglophone minority.

10 Oui ou Non?
Opinion on whether Quebec should split from Canada has evolved over the years. In a 1995 referendum held by the PQ, just 50.5 percent voted "no." Since then, support has fallen as the PQ drops in and out of power.

TOP 10 INDIGENOUS EXPERIENCES

Pow Wow dancers in Wendake

1 Pow Wow
In June, Wendake hosts a Pow Wow event with traditional dance and regalia.

2 Traditional Huron Onhoüa Chetek8e Site, Wendake
MAP P3 ▪ 575 Rue Chef Stanislas Koska
Learn about the history of the Huron nation and attend a handicraft workshop.

3 Chute Kabir Kouba, Quebec City
MAP P3
This park is an important heritage site for the Huron-Wendat peoples.

4 National Longhouse, Wendake
MAP P3 ▪ 15 Pl de la Rencontre
Sit around a fire pit and listen to a story-teller recite local myths and legends.

5 Notre-Dame de Lorette, Quebec City
MAP P3
This heritage site symbolizes the Christianization of the Huron-Wendats.

6 Hôtel-Musée Premières Nations, Wendake
MAP P3 ▪ 5 Pl de la Recontre
A hotel and museum exploring the history of the Huron-Wendat peoples.

7 Place Onywahtehretsih, Wendake
MAP P3
This square represents Huron-Wendat culture. It has a fountain with sculptures.

8 La Traite, Wendake
MAP P3 ▪ 5 Pl de la Rencontre
Indigenous cuisine is celebrated at this gourmet restaurant.

9 Hannenorak Library, Wendake
MAP P3 ▪ 87 Blvd Bastien
A bookstore with the largest selection of First Nations literature in Quebec City.

10 Restaurant Sagamité, Quebec City
MAP L5 ▪ 68 1/2 Rue Saint-Louis
Dine on delicious Indigenous dishes such as *sagamité* (hominy stew) here.

Cultural Québécois

Novelist Gabrielle Roy

the first popular singer-songwriter from Quebec. Today, a new generation of Quebecers enjoys her musical traditions.

1 Gabrielle Roy

Born in Manitoba to a French mother, and the youngest of 11 children, Roy (1909–83) escaped her family's poverty and moved to Quebec in 1939, where she began her career as a respected and prolific French-speaking novelist. Her first work, *Bonheur d'occasion (The Tin Flute)*, was published in 1945, winning her the Prix Fémina award and the first of three coveted Governor General's awards.

2 Émile Nelligan

Nelligan (1879–1941) was a romantic figurehead who ushered French-Canadian poetry into a new epoch and is revered by Quebecers as their beloved literary spokesman. In 1897 Nelligan joined the École Littéraire de Montréal and caused a triumphant public reaction to the reading of his poem "La Romance du Vin."

3 Mary Travers

Travers (1894–1941), born to an impoverished family on the Gaspé Peninsula, was a natural entertainer and began her career at family soirées playing jigs on the fiddle and spoons. Known as "La Bolduc," she rose to fame during the Great Depression to become

4 Paul-Émile Borduas

The painter Borduas (1905–60) is one of Quebec's most legendary artists and also one of its greatest political activists. Born in St-Hilaire, just outside Montreal, he made his name when he criticized the established social and political norms in 1948 by writing a scathing manifesto entitled *Refus Global*. He was a founding member of the abstract Automatistes school of art, which included Jean-Paul Riopelle.

5 Félix Leclerc

Leclerc (1914–88) worked as a radio announcer, actor, and comedian, but he is probably best remembered as a consummate storyteller, singer, and songwriter, penning works about the Canadian countryside, solitude, and love. His monument is found on Île d'Orléans, and a statue has been erected in his honor in Parc Lafontaine in Montreal (see p46).

6 Oscar Peterson

Peterson (1925–2007) entered an amateur talent contest aged 14 in his home town of Montreal – an event that he went on to win and which inspired him to leave high school and dedicate his life to jazz.

Oscar Peterson receiving a Grammy

A magical performance from circus troupe Cirque du Soleil

However his father only gave him permission to do so providing he worked to become the best jazz pianist in the world. Peterson succeeded beyond anyone's imagination: five unequalled decades of recordings are a testament to his virtuosity and have made him one of the greats of this musical genre.

7 Mordecai Richler

The Montreal novelist, essayist, and critic (1931–2001) was known for his sarcastic wit and biting opposition to Quebec's separatist elements. His most popular book, *The Apprenticeship of Duddy Kravitz* (1959), was adapted for film, launching Richard Dreyfuss to Hollywood stardom in 1974. Richler is best known for writing about greed and the human condition, as in *St Urbain's Horseman* (1971) and *Barney's Version* (1997), but he also wrote a number of humorous essays.

8 Leonard Cohen

A Montreal darling, Leonard Cohen (1934–2016) was born in Westmount to an affluent family. Once a poet and novelist, he began writing songs and recording music in the late 1960s. Cohen's music is soulful with slightly dark undertones. Today, a 26-story mural of Cohen can be found in Montreal's Golden Square Mile neighborhood.

9 Cirque du Soleil

This circus troupe was born as street performers in Baie-St-Paul, northeast of Quebec City. Employing a mix of stunning acrobatics, dazzling costumes, and inventive music, Cirque has become the most famous circus in the world. Headquartered in Montreal, Cirque has touring and resident shows in cities around the globe, most evident in Las Vegas.

Céline Dion in concert

10 Céline Dion

Dion (b.1968) was born into a musical family in Charlemagne. A demo tape made at 12 years old led to an agent, the late René Angélil, a recording contract, and eventually to her and Angélil's marriage. Today, Dion is one of the greatest Canadian artists in history, with record sales of over 250 million copies worldwide.

🔟 Historic Sites

Marché Bonsecours, one of Canada's finest heritage buildings

1 Marché Bonsecours, Montreal

This beautiful Neo-Classical domed structure was once home to Canada's parliament but is today used variously as a produce market, art gallery, concert venue, reception hall, and shopping mall, and is home to Quebec Crafts Council. The symmetrical gem of Vieux-Montréal features a Greek Revival portico and cast-iron columns made in the early 1800s (see p62).

2 La Citadelle, Quebec City

The colossal fortification was originally built by Royal Engineer Josué Dubois Berthelot de Beaucours in 1693. The complete star-shaped bastion seen today, however, is primarily the work of English Colonel Elias Durnford, constructed between 1820 and 1832 (see pp28–9).

3 Basilique Notre-Dame, Montreal

Once the largest church in North America, the imposing Gothic towers of the cathedral loom over Place d'Armes. The inside has a decorative nave composed of stained-glass windows, hand-carved wooden statues, ornate goldleaf trimmings, and paintings (see pp16–17).

4 Place Royale, Montreal
MAP K3

Montreal's oldest public square (1657) is located on the site where the city was originally founded in 1642. Small and easy to overlook, the square features the Pointe-à-Callière museum (see pp22–3), a gift shop, and outdoor events. The residence of Louis-Hector Callière, a French governor, was also once located here, as was the 19th-century Royal Insurance Building and Montreal's first Customs House.

5 Château Ramezay, Montreal

An elegant heritage museum sits across the street from the Hôtel de Ville in an 18th-century former

Elegant interior of Château Ramezay

governor's home. Artifacts from Indigenous societies through to the arrival of British and French colonizers up to 1900 are on display. The gift shop has unique souvenirs and the comfortable café terrace faces onto the Jardins du Gouverneur and Place Jacques-Cartier *(see p62)*.

Exhibit at Sir George-Étienne-Cartier National Historic Site

6 Sir George-Étienne-Cartier National Historic Site, Montreal

A Victorian home, restored by Parks Canada as a National Historic Site, contains marvelous interactive exhibitions inviting visitors into a typical 19th-century parlor. Enjoy theatrical re-enactments portrayed in shows such as "A Victorian Christmas," "A Servant Confides," and "Elegance and Propriety: Etiquette at the Cartiers," all of which offer a fascinating insight into the lives once lived here *(see p63)*.

7 Place Jacques-Cartier, Montreal

The magnetic center of Vieux-Montréal, this square offers a variety of stores, clubs and restaurants, while being enlivened by street performers and horse-drawn *calèche* rides. This is a wonderful spot to arrange meetings, take breaks from sightseeing, sit in the sun with a good book, or simply people-watch. Look out for an entertaining troupe called the Old Montreal Ghost Trail located just south of the square, who offer fascinating tours of the city's eerier past *(see p62)*.

8 Hôtel de Ville, Montreal

While visiting Montreal's World Fair in 1967, French president Charles de Gaulle made history from the balcony of this building by announcing *"Vive le Québec – Vive le Québec Libre!"* ("Long Live Quebec – Long Live Free Quebec"), proving his support for the province's separation from the rest of Canada *(see p31)*. Sign up for a guided tour to enjoy fully the grace of this historic town hall built in the Second Empire style *(see p61)*.

9 Parc des Champs-de-Bataille, Quebec City

This park commemorates the Battle of the Plains of Abraham *(see p40)*, in which the generals of both sides, English General Wolfe and French General Montcalm, died during a fierce engagement lasting less than 30 minutes. The element of surprise was on the side of the British as no army had ever before managed to scale the Cap Diamant escarpment. A visit to the Plains of Abraham Museum at 835 Rue Wilfrid-Laurier will explain more on this important event and its consequences for Canadian history *(see p94)*.

Iconic Château Frontenac

10 Château Frontenac, Quebec City

Among the most photographed hotels in the world, this elegant château poses majestically on the heights of Haute-Ville. Built by railroad tycoon Cornelius Van Horne, this hotel belongs to the Canadian Pacific railroad empire *(see p112)*.

🔟 Parks and Waterways

 Pôle-des-Rapides
MAP P6

This historic area originated from the drama of the Lachine Rapids, which prevented early explorers, settlers, traders, and the military from continuing farther west. It now includes the communities of Lachine, LaSalle, and Verdun, minutes from downtown Montreal. Featuring the most popular cycle path in Canada and 60 miles (100 km) of trails, the district is also home to the Fur Trade at Lachine National Historic Site.

2 Parc du Mont-Royal, Montreal

The largest and most inviting natural playground in Montreal is a year-round magnet for outdoor sports enthusiasts as well as leisure and relaxation buffs. Parc du Mont-Royal has a wealth of wildlife and bird species, as well as a lake, streams, hiking paths, summer cycling, and winter cross-country skiing trails, lookouts, an interpretation center, and a wonderful collection of original sculptures *(see pp12–13)*.

 Parc Maisonneuve, Montreal
Métro Viau

Situated within the Parc Olympique area *(see pp18–19)*, this huge chunk of greenery provide fun and leisure in the east of the city. Facilities include a nine-hole golf course in summer and a winter ice-skating rink.

Urban green space of Parc Lafontaine

4 Parc Lafontaine, Montreal
MAP E2

On the site of an old military armament range, attractive tree-lined pathways and shady spots are a perfect setting for many cultural events, celebrations, and community activities throughout the year. The park is a friendly neighborhood expanse containing a duck pond, cultural center, concert venue, and monuments honoring Québécois figures such as Félix Leclerc.

 Parc Jean-Drapeau, Montreal
MAP F5

Parc Jean-Drapeau is made up of Île Sainte-Hélène and Île Notre-Dame. Most visitors come here to attend

Biosphère, Parc Jean-Drapeau

the amusement park or the numerous festivals and fireworks displays held throughout the year.

6 Parc des Champs-de-Bataille, Quebec City

This is the city's largest and most scenic park. With over 250 acres (100 ha) of undulating hills and the St Lawrence River on the horizon, it's hard to believe that beautiful Battlefields Park has such a harsh military history. It was the site of the famed Battle of the Plains of Abraham in 1759, the events of which formed British Canada (see p94).

Parc des Champs-de-Bataille

7 Parc de la Francophonie, Quebec City

MAP K6

Created to commemorate the cultural alliance of 84 French-speaking governments and states, this peaceful park is dotted with ponds and fountains. It stands in stark contrast to the politically active area in which it lies, right beside the parliament building. This historic area was formerly known as Quartier St-Louis.

8 Parc du Cavalier du Moulin, Quebec City

MAP L5

At the western end of Rue Mont-Carmel sits a delightful park, where poets, lovers, and tourists enjoy the remarkable view of Avenue Sainte-Geneviève, the Chalmers-Wesley United Church, Hôtel du Parlement, La Citadelle, and the striking houses standing on Rue Saint-Louis.

9 Parc Montmorency, Quebec City

MAP M5

At this magnificent vantage point, overlooking the St Lawrence River, Alfred Laliberté, a Montreal sculptor, has created bronze memorials to many famous Canadians, including one of Sir George-Étienne Cartier, whose signature is on the Confederation Act of 1867. From here there are great views of the Séminaire de Québec.

10 Square Dorchester and Place du Canada, Montreal

MAP H2

This gracious square was the Catholic cemetery from 1798 to 1854 and is surrounded by elegant churches and buildings. Highlighted by the Sun Life Building on its east side, once the largest structure in the British Commonwealth, Square Dorchester contains numerous monuments, including one of the first French Canadian prime minister Sir Wilfrid Laurier, and is the starting point for city tours. Place du Canada has manicured gardens and was established to honor the nation's dead from both World Wars.

Place du Canada, Montreal

TOP 10 Outdoor Activities

Sightseeing tour boat

1 Boating, Canoeing, and Rafting

Jetboat excursions: 47 Rue de la Commune Ouest ▪ (514) 284 9607 ▪ www.jetboatingmontreal.com

These activities have always been an integral part of life in Montreal. Yachts and sailboats contribute to the colorful marine ambiance of the Vieux-Port in Montreal. Saute-Moutons is the premier Lachine Rapids jetboat (motorized rafting) excursion, departing from the Quai de l'Horlogue, while canoeing can be enjoyed on the Canal Lachine.

2 Hiking
MAP N5

Quebec rewards walkers. One of the province's many routes is Parc Linéaire Le P'tit Train du Nord – a former rail track that has now been turned into a 144-mile (232-km) trail. The train once took weekenders from Montreal to the part of the Laurentian mountains located at the southern end to Mont-Laurier on the northern extreme.

3 Swimming

There are more than 48 indoor pools in the Montreal area, including Olympic-size facilities at Parc Olympique (see pp18–19). In summer there is a beach on Île Notre-Dame, south of Vieux-Port, with a shop, restaurant, and picnic areas.

4 Skating and Snowshoeing

Indoor arenas in summer and outdoor city parks and lakes in winter provide numerous ice-skating options in both cities. Snowshoeing is reserved for larger areas such as Parc du Mont-Royal in Montreal.

5 Rappelling and Mountain Climbing

Sépaq: 1-800 665 6527 ▪ www.sepaq.com

These are two of the fastest growing adventure sports throughout Quebec, with a bevy of challenges available outside both cities. The vast mountainous expanses are overseen by Sépaq (Parks Québec).

6 Skiing

Quebec has hundreds of downhill skiing trails throughout the Laurentian, Adirondack, Green, and White Mountain ranges within hours of both cities. The Cantons-de-l'Est (see p87) offer excellent pistes at

Skiing in Les Laurentides

Mont Orford, while near Quebec City are ski runs at Mont Sainte-Anne (see p102). Cross-country legends abound in Quebec, with Herman "Jackrabbit" Johannsen at the top of the list. Montreal is filled with large parks ideal for cross-country skiing.

7 Snowmobiling

There are 20,690 miles (33,300 km) of marked, interconnected trails in the province of Quebec. From mid-December to mid-March, take a guided snowmobile tour or rent one on your own. In summer, these same trails are used for ATV/Quad excursions.

8 Biking

Montreal is criss-crossed with bike trails, including along the waterfront, and Quebec City offers unique pedaling paths through historic neighborhoods. The Cantons-de-l'Est have cycling trails past rolling hills and quiet rivers, with the snow-capped peaks beyond.

Biking in Montreal

9 Horse Riding

Ranch Mont-Tremblant: (819) 681 4848

West of Montreal is horse country; make a day of it by touring the rolling hills of Hudson and Rigaud (see p85). The Ranch Mont-Tremblant also has a network of trails.

10 Ziplining

Aerial forest adventures can be booked at Mont Tremblant, or try an urban zipline circuit over the Old Port of Montreal with MTL Zipline (see p64). In Quebec City, zipline across Montmorency Falls.

TOP 10 SPECTATOR SPORTS

Ice-hockey players in action

1 Les Canadiens de Montréal Club de Hockey
One of the world's most successful professional sports organizations attracts 21,000 fans to the Bell Centre for their famous ice-hockey battles.

2 Tournoi International de Hockey Pee-Wee de Québec
The largest youth ice-hockey tournament in the world.

3 Formula 1 in Montreal
The planet's fastest drivers tour the Circuit Gilles-Villeneuve in Montreal's annual F1 Grand Prix (see p56).

4 Québec Capitales Baseball
Can-Am League's best team plays at the Stade Canac in Quebec City.

5 Tour de l'Île de Montréal
The entire city turns out for this bicycle race where cyclists ride over a distance of 62 miles (100 km).

6 Montréal Alouettes Canadian Football
Founded in 1946, the Montréal Alouettes play at the Percival Molson Stadium. Their last Grey Cup win was in 2010.

7 Montreal Impact Soccer
Montreal's Impact is the city's main soccer team.

8 Parc Jarry Tennis Championships
Parc Jarry hosts international professional tennis events.

9 Grand Prix Cycliste de Montréal
During this one-day race, cyclists must climb and descend on a 7.5-mile (12-km) circuit that runs around Mont-Royal 17 times.

10 Montreal Marathon
Every September hundreds of runners take part in this race through the city.

TOP 10 Children's Attractions

One of the many hair-raising rides at La Ronde Six Flags Amusement Park

1 Centre des Sciences de Montréal

The underlying thrust of this center is to demystify all aspects of science, from technology and how it influences our daily lives, to exploring the under-water world of the ocean. Innovative interactive games make the learning fun. There is an indoor playground for younger kids with a life-size playhouse and large building blocks (see p64).

Centre des Sciences de Montréal

2 La Ronde Six Flags Amusement Park, Montreal

MAP F4 ■ 22 Chemin Macdonald, Île Ste-Hélène ■ (514) 397 2000 ■ Open May–Oct: daily ■ Adm ■ www.laronde.com

The largest amusement park in Quebec was originally opened for Expo '67. Six Flags took over as owner in 2001 and has added many rides since then. Le Monstre is the world's tallest two-track wooden roller coaster, perfect for thrill-seekers. Tamer rides, such as the family boats rides, mini-trains, and carousels, will appeal to younger children.

3 Insectarium, Montreal

MAP P6 ■ 4581 Rue Sherbrooke Est ■ Métro Viau, Pie-IX ■ (514) 868 3000 ■ Open daily (times vary, check website) ■ Adm ■ www. espacepourlavie.ca/insectarium

This astounding display celebrates insects of every size and shape. It opened in 1990 thanks to Georges Brossard, who traveled the world to collect the fascinating bugs. Although most of the insects are dead, there are live tarantulas and other creepy crawlies, safely ensconced behind glass (see p19).

4 Biodôme, Montreal

MAP P6 ■ 4777 Ave Pierre-de-Coubertin ■ Métro Viau ■ (514) 868 3000 ■ Adm ■ www.espacepourlavie. ca/biodome

It is rare to see birds from the northern and southern hemi-spheres in one place, but in this unusual exhibit, animals from the Arctic, Antarctic, Tropics, Laurentian, and St Lawrence marine habitats are housed under one roof in controlled settings to resemble their natural habitats (see p19).

5 Laser Quest, Montreal
MAP G1 ■ 1226 Rue Ste-Catherine Ouest ■ (514) 393 3000 ■ Open daily (times vary, call ahead to check); Mon for private groups only ■ Adm

Laser Quest adds a high-tech twist to the classic games of hide-and-seek and tag. The dark labyrinth of passageways in this multilevel arena feature fog, specilized lighting, and music. The aim is to find and tag your opponents as often as you can.

6 Planétarium Rio Tinto Alcan, Montreal
MAP P6 ■ 4801 Ave Pierre-De Coubertin ■ Métro Viau ■ (514) 868 3000 ■ Open 9am–5pm Tue–Sun (to 8pm Thu–Sat) ■ Adm ■ www.espace pourlavie.ca/planetarium

Here, visitors are propelled into the heavens courtesy of high-precision technology. A fascinating journey into time and outer space to make sense of the planets and the universe.

Planétarium Rio Tinto Alcan

7 Cosmodôme, Laval
MAP P6 ■ 2150 Laurentian Autoroute, Laval ■ (450) 978 3600 ■ Open daily ■ Adm ■ www.cosmodome.org

This museum and education center provides a fascinating look at space and the universe in all its diversity. Large-scale models of the solar system explain the make-up of every planet, while the rockets exhibition provides an insight into space travel.

8 Le Théâtre de L'Oeil, Montreal
MAP E1 ■ 911 Rue Jean-Talon Est, Suite 211B ■ (514) 278 9188 ■ Opening times vary, check website ■ Adm ■ www.theatre deloeil.qc.ca

Performances, workshops, and exhibitions are all part of the fun at this puppet theater. Kids can watch how the puppets are made, learn to pull their strings, and then attend a show.

Rocket exhibit, Cosmodôme

9 Biosphère, Montreal
Housed in Expo '67's iconic American pavilion designed by American architect Buckminster Fuller, the Biosphère (see p64) is intended to introduce children to environmental issues in an engaging and fun manner.

10 Arbraska, Mont-Saint-Grégoire
MAP P6 ■ 45 Chemin du Sous-Bois ■ Opening times vary, check website ■ Adm ■ www.arbraska.com

This adventure park has seven outposts in Quebec City. The Mont-Saint-Grégorie branch is located just a 30-minute drive from Montreal, making it easy to access from the city. The park offers plenty of entertain-ment for everyone, especially children over the age of five. Kids can spend the day ziplining through the trees, traversing suspension bridges, and tackling tree-top obstacle courses.

㊉ Performing Arts Venues

Auditorium, Théâtre de Quat'Sous

① Théâtre de Quat'Sous, Montreal

MAP D3 ▪ 100 Ave des Pins Est ▪ (514) 845 7277 ▪ www.quatsous.com

Set in a former synagogue, this brilliant French troupe has given many young performers, writers, and producers their first platform.

② Théâtre d'Aujourd'hui, Montreal

MAP E2 ▪ 3900 Rue St-Denis ▪ (514) 282 3900 ▪ www.theatredaujourdhui.qc.ca

A French theater company founded in 1968, committed to writing, staging, and producing Québécois plays. It is guided by the passion of artistic director Sylvain Bélanger.

③ Théâtre du Nouveau Monde, Montreal

MAP K1 ▪ 84 Rue Ste-Catherine Ouest ▪ (514) 866 8668 ▪ www.tnm.qc.ca

Begun in 1951, this is the heart of Québécois theater. The company moved to this heritage building in 1972 and has been putting on legendary shows ever since.

④ Place des Arts, Montreal

MAP K1 ▪ (514) 842 2112 ▪ www.placedesarts.com

The cultural centerpiece of Montreal. Five modern venues and an outdoor plaza stage countless performances and are permanent homes to the Orchestre Symphonique de Montréal, Opéra de Montréal, and Les Grands Ballets Canadiens de Montréal. It is also the home of the International Jazz Festival of Montreal, Festival FrancoFolies, and Festival Montréal en Lumière *(see pp56–7)*.

⑤ Grand Théâtre de Québec, Quebec City

MAP H6 ▪ 269 Blvd René-Lévesque Est ▪ (418) 643 8131 ▪ www.grandtheatre.qc.ca

Conceived by Canadian architect and urban theorist Victor Prus, this inventive space uses a stacked concert hall grid to overcome space limitations. Opened in 1971, the theater features a spectacular mural by Quebec artist Jordi Bonet, which leads to the Salle Louis-Fréchette and Octave-Crémazie concert halls. Théâtre du Trident, Opéra de Québec, and the Club Musical de Québec are based here, as well as the Orchestre Symphonique de Québec. Pop concerts are also staged here occasionally.

Production at Théâtre du Rideau Vert

⑥ Théâtre du Rideau Vert, Montreal

MAP E2 ▪ 4664 Rue St-Denis ▪ (514) 844 1793 ▪ www.rideauvert.qc.ca

For over 60 years (established in 1949) this French-speaking theater has had an outstanding reputation for the quality of its productions. The program offers everything from classics to contemporary works to international tours.

Le Capitole de Québec, illuminated during an evening performance

7 Le Capitole de Québec et Cabaret du Capitole, Quebec City

MAP K5 ■ 972 Rue St-Jean ■ (418) 694 4444 ■ www.theatrecapitole.com

Le Capitole is a testament to the committed preservation of historic buildings in Quebec City. Built in 1903 and refurbished by New York architect Thomas W. Lamb in the 1920s, it was given a third lease on life in the 1980s and is now the preferred showcase for theater, cabaret, and cultural events.

8 Théâtre du Petit Champlain Maison de la Chanson, Quebec City

MAP M5 ■ 68 Rue du Petit Champlain ■ (418) 692 2631 ■ www.theatrepetitchamplain.com

Perhaps the most compelling modern theater in the country is hidden on a crowded stretch of the Rue du Petit Champlain. The building is a beautiful balance of history and contemporary design; inside, the performance space is comfortable and the audience seating generous. The schedule has up-and-coming acts as well as established artists.

9 Théâtre de la Bordée, Quebec City

La Bordée has been producing shows since the 1970s and has always been a local favorite. Set in the refurbished Pigalle movie house in the Quartier St-Roch (see p98), this spacious, modern theater features 350 seats. Here, artistic director Michel Nadeau presents contemporary dramas with a touch of political realism. The company has also invited luminaries such as director Robert Lepage to mount original works.

10 Centaur Theatre, Montreal

MAP K3 ■ 453 Rue St-François-Xavier ■ (514) 288 1229 ■ www.centaur theatre.com

Montreal's principal English-language theatrical venue was founded in 1969. Housed in the Old Stock Exchange Building, it has two stages and is well-known for its world-class productions. The program varies between Broadway musicals and contemporary Canadian drama, as well as works by international playwrights.

Entrance to the Centaur Theatre

🔟 Montreal and Quebec City for Free

Quebec winter carnival sculpture

① Free Festivals

The festivals of Montreal and Quebec City feature a huge variety of free shows and performances, from stand-up comedy at Juste pour Rire (see p56) to jazz shows at Festival International de Jazz de Montréal (see p56) to winter fun at the Carnaval de Québec (see p57).

② Free Days at Museums

There is free admission to the permanent collection at Musée des Beaux-Arts de Montréal (see pp24–5) each day. During UNESCO's International Museum Day (late May), numerous other museums are free of charge from 9am until 6pm and provide a free shuttle bus. Check individual websites for details.

Musée des Beaux-Arts de Montréal

③ Tango Libre

www.tangolibre.ca

It may take two to tango, but in Montreal it also takes no money. The perennially popular Tango Libre offers free introductory classes, at various parks in the summer and in studios in the winter.

④ Maisons de la Culture

www.accesculture.com

Montreal's secret for free entertainment is the Maisons de la Culture network, which is a series of venues offering complimentary performances, from performing arts to photography, by local artists.

⑤ Church Concerts

www.montrealcathedral.ca, www.notre-dame-de-quebec.org

Numerous churches and cathedrals host free concerts, including the Christ Church Cathedral in Montreal and the Basilique-Cathédrale Notre-Dame-de-Québec in Quebec City. Also, you can celebrate Sunday mass at 11am at Montreal's Notre-Dame Basilica (see pp16–17) to the uplifting sounds of a choir.

⑥ City Parks

Montreal's Parc du Mont-Royal (see pp12–13), which elegantly presides over the city, abounds with free outdoor activities, from strolling the shaded paths to floating toy boats at Lac Aux Castor (Beaver Lake). Just northeast of Quebec City, explore the lush greenery and trickling streams of Parc Chauveau.

⑦ McGill University

Stroll through a Neo-Classical stone gate to enter McGill, Montreal's prestigious university, which is filled with free arts and culture. The Musée Redpath showcases a top-notch natural history collection and the campus is dotted with sculptures, notably Raymond Mason's *The Illuminated Crowd*. You can often catch free performances at the Schulich School of Music *(see p70)*.

Musée Redpath, McGill University

⑧ Free Walking Tours

www.freemontrealtours.com, www.afreetourofquebec.com

Explore both cities on free walking tours, like the Free Old Montreal Tour, a historical and cultural tour led by a local, and A Free Tour of Quebec.

⑨ Art Mûr Gallery, Montreal

5826 Rue St-Hubert ■ (514) 933 0711 ■ **Closed Sun–Mon** ■ www.artmur.com

Peruse contemporary art by award-winning artists from around Canada, and the world, at this free gallery.

⑩ Théâtre de Verdure

www.accesculture.com/contenu/theatredeverdure

This amphitheater, located in Montreal's Parc de la Fontaine, features a diverse array of free performances in summer that includes theater, dance, and music.

TOP 10 BUDGET TIPS

1 Wednesday evenings admission is free at the McCord Museum *(see p69)* and half-price at the MAC *(see p70)*.

2 Quebec City and Montreal are famous for cheap comfort food outlets, including *casse-croûtes* (snack bars).

3 *Friperies* (secondhand clothiers) sell fashions from every era and style at cheap prices. Rue St-Denis, Avenue Mont-Royal, Rue Ste-Catherine Est, and Boulevard St-Laurent in Montreal are good places to scout.

4 Sleep for cheap at youth hostels, including Samesun Montréal and the HI Quebec City.

5 Pick up the Passeport MTL card *(www.passeportmtl.com)*, which offers free access to key city attractions and unlimited use of public transport.

6 Nab same-day discount tickets to the symphony, opera, theater, comedy, and more through La Vitrine *(www.lavitrine.com)*, a ticket booth at Montreal's Place des Arts in downtown.

7 For a cheap night out, head to *apportez votre vin* ("bring your own wine") restaurants. Before dinner, enjoy the *cinq à sept* (5–7pm happy hour).

8 The Express Bus 747 *(www.stm.info)* is the cheapest ride between the airport and Montreal's city center.

9 Check the local papers for free or discounted entertainment; the Vieux-Port areas in both Montreal and Quebec City regularly present outdoor concerts and firework displays for free.

10 Munch on wedges of Québécois cheese, olives, warm bread rolls, and other complimentary local samples at Jean-Talon Market and Atwater Market in Montreal, and Le Grand Marché de Québec *(see p95)* in Quebec City.

Apples on sale, Jean-Talon Market

Festivals and Events

① Carnaval de Québec

Late Jan–Feb ▪ www.carnaval.qc.ca

Few events define Quebec City like the Carnaval de Québec, one of the largest winter festivals in the world. Among the festival highlights are the fairytale Palais de Glace (Ice Palace), which is constructed from 6,000 frozen blocks of ice; the International Snow Sculpture competition; parades; and Québécois food and drink, including Caribou, made with whisky, sherry, port, brandy, and maple sugar.

Bonhomme, the Carnaval mascot

② Festival Montréal en Lumière

www.montrealenlumiere.com

The spirits of Montrealers are given a boost during the winter months in this celebration of life through light. Each night over the festival's two-week run in February, organizers host a wild combination of attractions, from outdoor sound and light *(son et lumière)* productions, to indoor concerts, illuminated buildings, theater and dance performances, culinary soirées of traditional foods, and nightly fireworks. This is a spectacular time to be visiting the city.

③ Les FrancoFolies de Montréal

Jun ▪ www.francofolies.com

A wildly eclectic music festival celebrating all types of French music. Over 500,000 people attend concerts by groups far from the mainstream of North American culture, with styles ranging from hip-hop to creole, rap, swing and, of course, traditional French songs.

④ Grand Prix du Canada

www.gpcanada.ca

Montreal hosts the world's fastest drivers each year for its Formula 1 Grand Prix, drawing thousands of visitors from across the globe. The event is held at the Circuit Gilles-Villeneuve, named after the French-Canadian racing driver.

⑤ Festival d'Été de Québec

www.feq.ca

For ten exciting days each July, Quebec City becomes one mammoth outdoor music stage as performers flock from all over the world to perform countless styles of music. This enormous spectacle is the most spirited activity of the summer, with 500 shows and some 1,000 artists blasting out their sounds at over 15 different performance venues.

The Strumbellas perform live at the Festival d'Été de Québec

6 Just For Laughs Festival
www.hahaha.com

Over 1.5 million jolly patrons attend a banquet of mirth each year in July at Montreal's comedy festival (Juste pour Rire). From quirky free shows staged in the Quartier Latin streets to the constantly sold-out Club Series and Loto-Québec Galas, humor in all its forms is on offer from more than 600 international performers.

7 Le Festival International de Jazz de Montréal
Late Jun–Jul ■ www.montreal jazzfest.com

The world's largest jazz festival takes over the concourse at Place des Arts in downtown Montreal, as well as neighborhood clubs, restaurants, and parks. Each year several million visitors party for 11 days of free outdoor concerts and a wide variety of musical events involving internationally renowned musicians.

L'International des Feux Loto-Québec

8 L'International des Feux Loto-Québec
Wed & Sat: 10pm ■ www.laronde.com

From early July to early August the skies over Vieux-Montréal light up twice a week with explosive theatrics for the Montreal Fireworks Festival, held at La Ronde amusement park (see pp50–51). Countries from around the world participate in this display of pyrotechnic talents, which is recognized as one of the most prestigious in the world. The beautiful fireworks are best viewed from the stands at La Ronde.

Fêtes de la Nouvelle-France

9 Fêtes de la Nouvelle-France
www.nouvellefrance.qc.ca

A large-scale voyage back in time transforms Place Royale and the Basse-Ville section of Quebec City into a magical melange of period costumes, traditional music and dance, and local cuisine, all to celebrate the settling of the city by the French in the 1600s (see p40). Early August crowds are invited to attend over 600 performances by local actors, musicians, dancers, and artists.

10 Rendez-vous ès TRAD
www.cvpv.net

A superb multicultural festival each fall at Chapelle du Musée de l'Amérique Francophone in Vieux-Québec (see p30) offers a sensuous feast of traditional music, dance, crafts, foods, and laughter. Share homespun hilarity while watching teams joust during joute chantée (an improvised singing tournament), or during the culinary fun of souper chanté (singing supper). Singers come from as far afield as Guatemala, Japan, Greece, Martinique, and Senegal.

Montreal and Quebec City Area by Area

Colorful Mont Tremblant Village in Les Laurentides during fall

Vieux-Montréal and Vieux-Port	**60**
Downtown and Quartier Latin	**68**
Mont-Royal to Hochelaga-Maisonneuve	**78**
Excursions from Montreal	**84**
Quebec City	**92**

☰10 Vieux-Montréal and Vieux-Port

This enchanting area, established in 1642, is a rewarding spot to begin a tour of the city of Montreal. Its ancient churches, cobblestone streets, and the bustling international port characterize this fascinating neighborhood. Vieux-Montréal epitomizes the romance, culture, and *joie-de-vivre* of the metro-polis, while the activity of mega-freighters and cruise boats in the Vieux-Port reveals that Montreal is the shipping gateway to the Great Lakes. The old quarter combines high-tech novelty with old-world charm as well as some of the city's best dining options. Plan to spend several days exploring the craft shops, museums,

Statue atop Notre-Dame-de-Bon-Secours

cultural exhibitions, and French bistros while savoring the European-style yet informal Québécois hospitality.

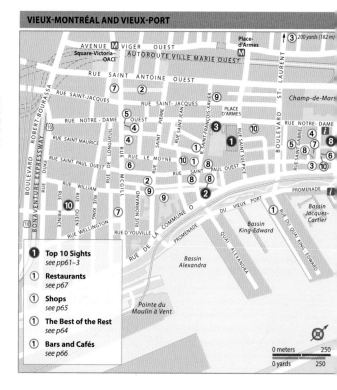

VIEUX-MONTRÉAL AND VIEUX-PORT

	Top 10 Sights see pp61–3
①	**Restaurants** see p67
①	**Shops** see p65
①	**The Best of the Rest** see p64
①	**Bars and Cafés** see p66

Basilique Notre-Dame altar

1 Basilique Notre-Dame

When the largest bell in North America begins to thunder over Place d'Armes, legions of pigeons create a spectacle reminiscent of St Peter's Square in Rome. Meanwhile throngs of pilgrims and visitors flock daily to this compelling architectural masterpiece (see pp16–17).

2 Pointe-à-Callière

This striking modern building, married with the ancient Place Royale setting, vibrates with activity throughout the year, as visitors digest one cultural exhibition treat after another on display inside and outside this museum (see pp22–3).

3 Séminaire St-Sulpice

MAP K3 ▪ 116 Rue Notre-Dame Ouest ▪ (514) 849 6561

Erected between 1685 and 1687 for the Sulpician religious order, the St Sulpice Seminary is the second oldest surviving building in Montreal. This remarkable historic edifice remains an icon of the institutional architecture that was employed in Nouvelle-France. The Sulpicians' clock above the main doorway is one of the oldest of its kind in North America, dating from 1701 (see p17). Closed to the public, the Seminary occasionally offers tours in the summer.

Montreal's Hôtel de Ville

4 Hôtel de Ville

MAP L2 ▪ 275 Rue Notre-Dame Est ▪ Open 8am–5pm Mon–Fri

The town hall was a gracious Second Empire-style edifice built between 1872 and 1878 by architect Henri-Maurice Perrault (1828–1903). Damaged by fire in 1922, it was rebuilt a year later in Beaux-Arts style, and is still used for its original function. You can visit the interior and free guided tours are offered in the summer. It is best seen at night when it illuminates the sky (see p45).

The stately Marché Bonsecours from across the Bassin Bonsecours

⑤ Marché Bonsecours

MAP L3 ■ 350 Rue St-Paul Est
■ **Open** 10am–6pm daily (to 9pm Jun–Sep; other late shopping evenings vary according to season)

This greystone Neo-Classical building has a rich history. It once housed the Parliament of Canada and was even a theatrical venue for Charles Dickens when he acted at the Théâtre Royal in 1842. Today it is a shopping center that attracts a continuing influx of visitors under its shining dome (see p44).

⑥ Place Jacques-Cartier and Place de la Dauversière

MAP L3

Two famous names in Canadian history have beautiful squares across from each other. Place Jacques-Cartier (see p45) celebrates the first Frenchman who reached Canada (see p40), while Place de la Dauversière honors Jerome le Royer, Sieur de la Dauversière of La Flèche in Anjou, France, the Royal Tax Collector whose idea it was to build a colony here, eventually called Ville-Marie.

⑦ Musée Marguerite-Bourgeoys and Chapelle Notre-Dame-de-Bon-Secours

MAP L3 ■ 400 Rue St-Paul Est ■ (514) 282 8670 ■ **Open** Tue–Sun (opening times vary, check website) ■ Adm ■ www.margueritebourgeoys.org

In 1653 Marguerite Bourgeoys arrived in Ville-Marie to open a school, which began in a stable assigned to her by the Sieur de Maisonneuve. By 1655 she was head of the Congregation of the Sisters of Notre-Dame and oversaw the construction of Canada's first stone church in 1675. The chapel that remains dates from 1771. It is known as the "Sailors Chapel," given its portside location and model ships hanging throughout.

⑧ Musée Château Ramezay

MAP L3 ■ 280 Rue Notre-Dame Est ■ (514) 861 3708 ■ **Open** Jun–Oct: 9:30am–6pm daily; Nov–May: 10am–4:30pm Tue–Sun ■ Adm ■ www.chateauramezay.qc.ca

This elegant stone home was constructed to house the Governor of Montreal, Claude de Ramezay (1659–1724), and his 16 children. It was thereafter known as the Maison des Castors (beavers) because it was home to the Compagnie des Indes (West Indies Company) and their burgeoning fur trade with Europe.

THE FRENCH ARRIVAL AND THE FUR TRADE

The original Huron village of Hochelaga (meaning "where the rivers meet") provided the French explorers with an ideal location from which to settle the new continent and the key staging area for exploration of the rest of North America. It also allowed access to the Huron fur-trading networks, resulting in an enormously profitable fur trade between Canada and Europe.

In 1775 General Richard Montgomery lived here with his band of American troops while they made a failed attempt to capture the city for the US. It has been a museum since 1895, illustrating the early settlement of Quebec, from tools to uniforms to historic documents. Of note is the Nantes Salon, lavishly decorated by 18th-century French architect, Germain Boffrand (see p44).

9 Sir George-Étienne-Cartier National Historic Site

MAP L3 ▪ 458 Rue Notre-Dame Est ▪ (514) 283 2282 ▪ Open Jun–Dec (opening times vary, check website) ▪ Adm ▪ www.pc.gc.ca

Preserved artifacts of the 19th-century upper-middle classes and their lifestyle are exhibited at Sir George-Étienne-Cartier's house. Cartier was one of the Fathers of Canadian Confederation and his home, where he lived from 1848 to 1871, provides an insight into the daily life of his social class at that time (see p45).

Sir George-Étienne-Cartier's home

10 Darling Foundry

MAP J3 ▪ 745 Rue Ottawa ▪ (514) 392 1554 ▪ Open noon–7pm Wed–Sun (to 10pm Thu) ▪ Adm ▪ www.fonderiedarling.org

This art space, which is housed in a converted foundry building, is home to changing exhibitions by visiting artists, with a focus on contemporary art. The Foundry also hosts openings and readings. It is the center of an expanding creative network, the Quartier Éphémère, in this former industrial district. Free on Thursdays.

AN AFTERNOON STROLL ALONG THE WATERFRONT

▶ **AFTERNOON**

Start your walk with a visit to the **Darling Foundry**, a cavernous contemporary art space at the western edge of Vieux-Montréal. Located on a small street in a warren of former industrial buildings, it contains some impressive works from Quebec and international artists that are worth the detour. Afterwards, walk over to Rue McGill and pop into the sleek and chic resto-boutique **Le Cartet** at No. 106 for a delicious lunch that can be eaten on-site or taken with you. Their coffee is fantastic, too.

Next, head east along the waterfront where you may find secondhand booksellers, yachts of the rich and famous, and portrait artists vying for your attention. Stay beside the water, past the **Centre des Sciences de Montréal** (see p64) to **Bassin Bonsecours**, the waterfall, and **Quai de l'Horloge** (see p64).

Go north to the **Chapelle Notre-Dame-de-Bon-Secours** (400 Rue St-Paul Est) where, if you are feeling energetic, you can climb the interior stairs for a wonderful view of the Vieux-Port, then go up Rue Bonsecours and turn left on Rue de Notre-Dame, where you'll see the patisserie **bar à beurre** (348 Rue de Notre-Dame Est). Try a boule de buerre (chocolate ball).

End your walk by strolling through **Marché Bonsecours**, with its designer boutiques, then continue along Rue St-Paul and start the evening with a cocktail on the **Hôtel Nelligan**'s rooftop, which has breathtaking views (see p114).

See map on pp60–61

The Best of the Rest

1 Centre des Sciences de Montréal
MAP K3 ▪ Quai King-Edward ▪ (514) 496 4724 ▪ Open 9am–4pm Mon–Fri, 10am–5pm Sat & Sun ▪ Adm ▪ www.centredessciences demontreal.com

This science and technology center offers quality entertainment for kids (and adults) with its games, IMAX theater, and interactive exhibits *(see p50)*.

2 Place Gare Viger
MAP M2 ▪ 755 Berri St ▪ www.placegareviger.com

Built in 1898 as a railway hotel and station, Place Gare Viger today combines the original château with modern buildings, creating a complex of offices, apartments, and a boutique hotel.

3 Plage de l'Horloge
MAP M3

In summer, this beach has comfy chairs, large colorful umbrellas, and a bistro. The rest of the year, enjoy the boardwalk and soak in the view of the skyline. No swimming allowed.

Silky sands at Plage de l'Horloge

4 Quai de l'Horloge
MAP M3

Climb the interior stairs of this 1922 clock tower for views over the port.

5 MTL Zipline
MAP L3 ▪ Hangar 16, 363 Rue de la Commune Est ▪ (514) 947 5463 ▪ Open May–Oct: 10am–10pm daily

This urban zipline circuit offers visitors a bird's-eye view of the city, beginning at the Vieux-Port.

Biosphère at Parc Jean-Drapeau

6 Biosphère
MAP F5 ▪ 160 Chemin Tour-de-l'Isle, Ile Ste-Hélène ▪ (514) 283 5000 ▪ Opening times vary, call ahead to check ▪ Adm

An architectural centerpiece created for Expo '67, the dome now acts as an Ecowatch Centre and a museum dedicated to the St Lawrence River and Great Lakes *(see p51)*.

7 Square Victoria
MAP J2

In 1860 a magnificent monument to honor Queen Victoria was erected on this haymarket square.

8 Old Customs House
This archetypal example of 1830s Neo-Classical architecture is today incorporated into the Pointe-à-Callière site *(see p23)*.

9 Bank of Montreal Museum
MAP K2 ▪ 129 Rue St-Jacques Ouest ▪ Open 10am–4pm Mon–Fri

The oldest bank in Canada (1817) houses an interesting currency museum within an ornate interior.

10 Lévis Tower
MAP F4 ▪ 221 Chemin Tour-de-l'Isle, Ile Ste-Hélène

Built in 1937 as part of the development of Ile Sainte-Hélène, this tower offers incredible views of downtown Montreal.

Shops

1 Marché Bonsecours
A Vieux-Montréal heritage landmark is now a bustling area of designer boutiques *(see p62)*.

2 Centre de Commerce Mondial
MAP J2 ■ 747 Rue du Square-Victoria

An inspiring architectural concept has been created by interlinking Ruelle des Fortifications heritage structures under a spectacular glass atrium. Shops, restaurants, offices, and a hotel can all be found here.

3 Galerie Michel-Ange
MAP L3 ■ 430 Rue Bonsecours

A reliable art gallery featuring many fine Québécois and international painters, which is located in a heritage house built in 1864.

4 Galerie le Chariot
MAP L3 ■ 446 Place Jacques-Cartier

A wonderful Inuit art collection awaits souvenir hunters in this gallery on Place Jacques-Cartier. One of the first businesses to preserve buildings in the Old Town, Galerie Le Chariot has treasures that will suit all budgets.

5 Camtec Photo
MAP J3 ■ 495 Rue McGill

Probably one of the last camera shops in the city, this is the place for all your photography needs. Vintage equipment as well as brand new gear can be found here. They even have their own laboratory on the premises.

6 Conseil des Métiers d'Art du Québec
MAP L3 ■ 390 Rue St-Paul Est

A sensational cooperative featuring Québécois artists working with varied materials. Choose from paintings, prints, and jewelry to clothing, toys, cards, glasswork, marionettes, and other fabulous gifts.

7 Le Cartet Boutique Alimentaire
MAP J3 ■ 106 Rue McGill

Drop in at this culinary emporium for the most delicious treats and foodstuffs. With goodies from around the planet, this tempting shop will set your senses ablaze.

8 Denis Gagnon
MAP K3 ■ 170 Rue St-Paul Ouest

This *enfant terrible* of the Quebec fashion scene has been wowing international audiences for years with his original and daring designs.

9 Espace Pepin
MAP J3 ■ 350 Rue St-Paul Ouest

With a natural vibe, this art concept store offers locally and ethically designed clothing and home decor.

10 Noël Eternel
MAP K3 ■ 60A Rue Notre-Dame Ouest

A store dedicated to the idea of keeping the Christmas spirit alive throughout the year. Stock up on unusual hand-crafted adornments, wrapping paper, stockings, games, dolls, and lots more.

Noël Eternel's sparkling display

See map on pp60–61

Bars and Cafés

① Clandestino
MAP K3 ▪ 436 Rue Saint Francois Xavier ▪ (514) 285 4037

An underground bar serving excellent mezcal- and tequilia-based cocktails. It has over 100 liquor varieties and 15 different kinds of salt. The bar itself has an eclectic, speakeasy vibe, making it the perfect evening getaway.

Cocktails at Maison St Paul

② Maison St Paul
MAP L3 ▪ 343 Rue St-Paul Est ▪ www.maisonsaintpaul.ca

Toast the night at this buzzy bar that celebrates bubbly in all its glory, from French Champagne to Spanish cava. Enjoy creative cocktails and tasty nibbles, like duck carpaccio with fig.

③ Le Mal Nécessaire
MAP K2 ▪ 1106 B Blvd St-Laurent ▪ www.lemalnecessaire.com

For Polynesian cocktails and delicious Chinese fusion, try this stylish tiki bar in Chinatown.

④ Santos
MAP L3 ▪ 191 Rue St-Paul Oest ▪ www.ilovesantos.ca

For a relaxed evening in Vieux-Montréal, head to laid-back Santos, where you can sample unusual tapas-style foods. Listen to live jazz during the week, and DJs play on weekends.

⑤ L'Auberge Saint-Gabriel
MAP K3 ▪ 426 Rue St-Gabriel ▪ www.aubergesaint-gabriel.com

One of the oldest inns in North America (1688) is now a bar-restaurant set in a romantic location. The popular Velvet bar offers an extensive wine selection.

⑥ The Coldroom
MAP L3 ▪ Rue Saint-Vincent ▪ www.thecoldroommtl.ca

Finding this basement speakeasy is part of the fun – all you have to do is follow the ducks. Here gourmet cocktails are accompanied by hearty appetizers such as hummus with warm pita bread and spicy sausages.

⑦ Bevo
MAP L3 ▪ 410 Rue St-Vincent ▪ www.bevopizza.com

Tucked away in a historic building on a tiny street, this bar serves traditional wood-fired pizzas while DJs spin on the weekends.

⑧ Stash Café
MAP K3 ▪ 200 Rue St-Paul Oest ▪ www.restaurantstashcafe.ca

A favorite actors' hangout near the Centaur Theatre (see p53), this Polish café-restaurant has a superb kitchen serving hearty *borscht* soup, with live piano music in the evenings.

⑨ Pub BreWskey
MAP L3 ▪ 380 Rue St-Paul Ouest ▪ www.brewskey.ca

This pub brews its own craft beers, plus serves whiskies and cocktails. The kitchen stays open until 3am and the patio is perfect for warm days.

Outdoor seating at Pub BreWskey

⑩ El Pequeño Bar
MAP L3 ▪ 401A Rue St-Vincent ▪ (514) 294 6911

El Pequeño is renowned for its classic Cuban cocktails and being the smallest cocktail bar in Canada.

Restaurants

PRICE CATEGORIES
For a three-course meal for one with half
a bottle of wine (or equivalent meal),
taxes and extra charges.

$ under $40 $$ $40–$80 $$$ over $80

1 Garde Manger
MAP K3 ■ 408 Rue St-François-
Xavier ■ (514) 678 5044 ■ www.garde
manger.ca ■ $$$

This upscale seafood spot is owned
by the Montreal celebrity chef Chuck
Hughes. Try the lobster risotto or,
for the more gluttonous, the famed
lobster *poutine (see p111)*.

2 Olive & Gourmando
MAP J3 ■ 351 Rue St-Paul
Ouest ■ (514) 350 1083 ■ www.
oliveetgourmando.com ■ $

Delightful and rustic, this bakery is
known for its brunch. It also serves
pastries, grilled paninis, and salads.

3 Pincette
MAP L3 ■ 94 Rue St-Paul Est
■ (514) 876 4261 ■ www.pincettemtl.
com ■ $$$

A new addition to Vieux-Montréal,
this is the place to go for all things
lobster – grilled lobster, lobster
poutine, lobster mac and cheese,
and more.

4 Boris Bistro
MAP J3 ■ 465 Rue McGill
■ (514) 848 9575 ■ www.boris
bistro.com ■ $$

A sensational mix is on the menu
here – sit in the lush garden and
try French fries cooked in duck
fat or divine poached salmon.

5 Club Chasse et Pêche
MAP L3 ■ 423 Rue St-Claude
■ (514) 861 1112 ■ www.leclub
chasseetpeche.com ■ $$$

This high-end restaurant, housed
in an attractive low, red-brick building, serves a robust mix of fresh
seafood and hearty meat dishes
in an intimate dining space.

Sophisticated dining at Holder

6 Holder
MAP J3 ■ 407 Rue McGill
■ (514) 849 0333 ■ www.
restaurantholder.com ■ $$

This elegant Holder brothers
restaurant-brasserie exudes
flair and good taste.

7 Loam
MAP J3 ■ 400 Rue Notre
Dame Est ■ (514) 662 5626 ■ $$

Known for its great ambience,
this trendy restaurant and bar has
an Art Deco vibe. The menu features
mostly French food, with classics
such as duck confit.

8 Restaurant Solmar
MAP L3 ■ 111 Rue St-Paul Est
■ (514) 861 4562 ■ www.solmar-
montreal.com ■ $$

A Portuguese mainstay renowned
for its lobster, steaks, and squid.

9 Gibby's
MAP K3 ■ 298 Place d'Youville
■ (514) 282 1837 ■ www.gibbys.com
■ $$$

One of Canada's finest eateries, with
a courtyard garden and a menu that's
big on oysters and steak.

10 Mandy's
MAP K3 ■ 425 Rue St-Nicolas
■ (514) 379 1979 ■ $

A create-your-own salad bar,
Mandy's has several locations
across Montreal. If it is cold out,
opt for the soup.

See map on pp60–61

TOP 10 Downtown and Quartier Latin

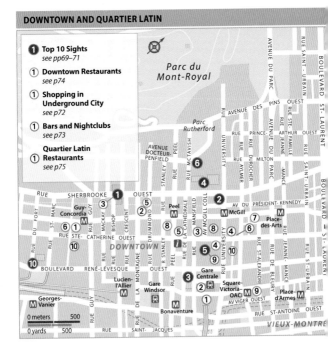

The two most animated and colorful areas of central Montreal, Downtown and Quartier Latin offer a cornucopia of delights. Though tiny by many mega-city standards, these *quartiers* (districts) are intriguing components of Montreal's urban landscape, bustling with activity around the clock. They are both home to many artists, designers, musicians, writers, and academics, as well as students from Concordia and McGill universities, all of whom are attracted by the eclectic mélange of historic sights, wonderful museums, LGBTQ+ venues, diverse restaurants and enclaves, colorful bars, and entrepreneurial businesses. No visit to Montreal would be complete without spending at least a couple of days exploring these two magnetic areas of the city.

Figure, Musée Redpath

DOWNTOWN AND QUARTIER LATIN

1. **Top 10 Sights**
   see pp69–71

1. **Downtown Restaurants**
   see p74

1. **Shopping in Underground City**
   see p72

1. **Bars and Nightclubs**
   see p73

1. **Quartier Latin Restaurants**
   see p75

Musée des Beaux-Arts

① Musée des Beaux-Arts

One of the oldest Canadian bastions of visual and decorative arts. The museum houses vast permanent collections and visiting exhibitions heralding the accomplishments of contemporary artists, as well as creative works by masters from other eras *(see pp24–5)*.

② McCord Museum

MAP J1 ▪ 690 Rue Sherbrooke Ouest ▪ (514) 861 6701 ▪ Open 10am–6pm Tue–Fri (to 9pm Wed), 10am–5pm Sat & Sun ▪ Adm ▪ www.musee-mccord.qc.ca

The single most important First Nations collection of artifacts in Quebec is on display at the McCord Museum, and includes the most extensive library of costumes and textiles in Canada. A particularly thrilling attraction is the Notman Photographic Archives, which records life in Montreal, Quebec, and Canada from 1840 to 1935. Over one million pictures are preserved and identified in more than 200 albums, which experts around the world use for research.

③ Cathédrale Marie-Reine-du-Monde

MAP H2 ▪ 1085 Rue de la Cathédrale ▪ Open 7am–7pm Mon–Fri, 7:30am–7pm Sat & Sun

Reminiscent of Saint Peter's Basilica in Rome, the cathedral was built in the 19th century to service the local Catholic community. It continues to attract visitors and residents, not least because of outstanding architectural features such as the Neo-Baroque copper and gold baldachin above the altarpiece. This church remains firmly at the heart of Montreal's downtown activity.

Cathédrale Marie-Reine-du-Monde

Exhibition hall, Musée Redpath

 McGill University

MAP J1 ▪ 845 Rue Sherbrooke Ouest

The campus spreads out over 80 lush acres (32 ha) of the downtown district. The land was a bequest from Scottish fur-trader James McGill in 1821 and was chartered by King George IV. Fine examples of Victorian architecture mix easily with the contemporary bustle of student life, making the 300 buildings on campus a testament to McGill's personal dream and a city's passion for education – McGill's School of Medicine is one of the finest.

 Musée d'Art Contemporain de Montréal

MAP K1 ▪ 1 Place Ville Marie ▪ (514) 847 6226 ▪ Open 11am–6pm Tue–Sun (to 9pm Wed) ▪ Adm ▪ www.macm.org

Dedicated solely to contemporary art, this high-profile institution has an innovative program of exhibitions highlighting the work of artists from Canada and the international circuit.

 Musée Redpath

MAP C3 ▪ 859 Rue Sherbrooke Ouest ▪ Open 9am–5pm Mon–Fri, 11am–5pm Sun ▪ www.mcgill.ca/redpath

The museum was opened in 1882 to house the collections of Sir William Dawson, a noted Canadian natural scientist. Part of McGill's Faculty of Science, it now displays biological, geological, and cultural artifacts. The building is also notable – built in 1880, it is steeped in Victorian Classicism and Greek Revival architecture.

7 Chinatown

MAP L2

Canada's transcontinental railway system owes a great debt to the many Chinese laborers who made it a reality. After 1880, when the railway was finished, Chinese workers decided to settle in Montreal and gathered together in this enclave to protect themselves against local discrimination. Today the area is also home to many other Southeast Asian communities. A stroll through the lantern-lit streets around Boulevard

The large campus of the Musée d'Art Contemporain de Montréal

Saint-Laurent and Rue de la Gauchetière reveals bargain boutiques and inexpensive restaurants.

8 Chapelle Notre-Dame-de-Lourdes

MAP L1 ▪ 430 Rue Ste-Catherine Est ▪ (514) 845 8278 ▪ Open 11am–6pm Mon–Fri, 10:30am–6:30pm Sat, 9am–6:30pm Sun ▪ www.cndlm.org

This richly decorated chapel, erected in 1876 for the Sulpician Order, is the greatest achievement of artist Napoleon Bourassa, grandson of Louis-Joseph Papineau, leader of the reformist Patriote movement. Bourassa studied in Paris, Rome, and Venice, returning to Montreal with the desire to create fine art as an expression of patriotism and faith.

9 Gay Village

MAP M1

Montreal is an LGBTQ+-friendly city, and one of the most festive parades belongs to this community. Between Rue St-Hubert and Avenue Papineau, the Village is alive around the clock. Restored homes mix with contemporary condominiums to create a diverse and exciting area.

Rue Ste-Catherine Est in Gay Village

10 Canadian Centre for Architecture

MAP B4 ▪ 1920 Rue Baile ▪ (514) 939 7026 ▪ Open 11am–6pm Wed–Sun (to 9pm Thu) ▪ Adm (except Thu evenings) ▪ www.cca.qc.ca

Opened in 1979 to build public awareness about architecture, the center promotes scholarly research in the field and stimulates innovation in design practice. Its collections include models, drawings, and photographs of some of the world's most important buildings.

AN AFTERNOON WALK THROUGH CHINATOWN AND QUARTIER LATIN

 AFTERNOON

Start at **St Patrick's Basilica** (corner of Rue St-Alexandre and Blvd René-Lévesque Ouest) to explore the nave of this wonderful church, then take Rue de la Gauchetière east across to **Avenue Viger Ouest**. Notice the beautiful Chinese lantern streetlights while you continue on to the bargain shops, dim sum restaurants, fresh produce markets, and herbal stores.

Head to **Boulevard St-Laurent**, the lively heart of Chinatown and the main street dividing Montreal into east and west. Stop at the corner of Boulevard St-Laurent and **Boulevard Renée-Lévesque** and gaze up at a huge mural that marks one of the entrances to Chinatown. Stroll to **Le Mal Nécessaire** (see p66), a subterranean tiki bar, for Hawaii-inspired drinks.

Make your way to **Rue St-Denis** and turn left. You now get to savor the effervescence of the Quartier-Latin, with its boutiques, restaurants, bistros, and cafés. Pop into any one of the strip's small shops, or rest and have a drink or snack on the huge front and back terraces of **Bar Le Saint-Sulpice** (see p73). Continue north to **Carré St-Louis**, the center of the quarter, with a distinctly French ambiance. Beautiful belle époque homes abound in this area, especially on **Avenue Laval**.

Continue the French theme for dinner on the terrace of **Café Cherrier** (see p75).

See map on pp68–9

Shopping in Underground City

1 Le 1000
MAP J2 ■ 1000 Rue de la Gauchetière Ouest

Inside Montreal's tallest building, under a glass dome, visitors will find an indoor skating rink surrounded by shops, fast food counters, and a gym.

2 Place Alexis Nihon
1500 Ave Atwater

With a good-value food court, plus direct access to the metro, this shopping mall has it all. The variety of stores here include a pharmacy, multiple big brand clothing stores and a department store.

3 Place Montréal Trust
MAP J1 ■ 1500 Ave McGill College

Place Montréal Trust has the highest spouting water fountain in North America at 100 ft (30 m), exclusive fashion outlets, and a large food court.

4 Promenades Cathédrale
MAP J1 ■ 625 Rue Ste-Catherine Ouest

This remarkable underground shopping concourse, consisting of 60 stores and restaurants, is built beneath the Christ Church Cathedral (1859).

5 Les Cours Mont-Royal
MAP H1 ■ 1455 Rue Peel

At the western end of the central shopping network, this attractive mall has the distinction of being set in the 1920s Mont-Royal Hotel, presenting elegant shops over four levels above and below ground.

6 La Baie
MAP J1 ■ 585 Rue Ste-Catherine Ouest

Also known as Hudson's Bay Company and The Bay in the rest of the country, this is a historic Canadian department store. You will find all the standard fare here, from fashion and accessories to household goods.

7 Complexe Desjardins
MAP K1 ■ 150 Rue Ste-Catherine Ouest

Standing across from the Place des Arts, this predominantly French mall is connected to Complex Guy-Favreau and Chinatown via underground tunnels.

Centre Eaton shopping mall

8 Centre Eaton
MAP J1 ■ 705 Rue Ste-Catherine Ouest

A light-filled glass cavern forms the entrance to this multilayered shopping and dining mall. The center also stages fashion and art events.

9 Place Ville-Marie
MAP J1 ■ 1 Place Ville-Marie

Place Ville-Marie attracts consumers in large numbers, but an additional bonus is its tranquil, leafy outdoor square – a summer lunchtime oasis.

10 Faubourg Sainte-Catherine
MAP G1 ■ 1616 Rue Ste-Catherine Ouest

Located in the heart of Shaughnessy Village this colorful glass mall is known for its fresh market produce and inexpensive eateries.

Bars and Nightclubs

1 Club Stéréo
MAP M1 ■ 858 Rue Ste-Catherine Est
One of the most powerful audio systems in any club in North America continues to pack this after-hours dance floor. A cross section of music styles attracts party animals.

2 Bar Cloakroom
MAP J1 ■ 2175 Rue de la Montagne
A cozy, kind-of-hidden, bespoke speakeasy that has no official menu. Let the master mixologists make you what you want.

3 Pub l'Ile Noir
MAP L1 ■ 1649 Rue St-Denis
A Scottish pub with wood decor and an excellent selection of single malt scotches and imported draught beer. The summer patio is great for people-watching.

4 Complexe Sky
MAP M1 ■ 1478 Rue Ste-Catherine Est
This amazingly large complex features a pub, a dance club, and a cabaret to entertain the large and growing LBGTQ+ community on the east side of downtown.

Outdoor seating, Les 3 Brasseurs

5 Les 3 Brasseurs
MAP L1 ■ 1658 Rue St-Denis
A lively location that opens onto Rue St-Denis on two sides with a superb terrace overlooking the flow of festivities. Serves wholesome cuisine and home-brewed beer.

Drinks being poured at La Distillerie No. 1

6 La Distillerie No. 1
MAP L1 ■ 300 Rue Ontario Est
Sip seasonal cocktails – like La Mere Amère, with amaretto, vodka, and grapefruit – from mason jars at this trendy bar. Refuel with fun bar snacks, including jars of gold-fish crackers and buttery popcorn.

7 Randolph Pub
MAP L1 ■ 2041 Rue St-Denis
Friendly spot with an expansive collection of ready-to-play board games on the shelves. Good beer and snack menu as well.

8 Pub Quartier-Latin
MAP L1 ■ 318 Rue Ontario Est
One of the most comfortable bars in town. There's a lovely terrace, a cozy bar, and a fabulous array of imported and domestic beer.

9 Pub Le Sainte-Élisabeth
MAP L2 ■ 1412 Rue Ste-Elisabeth
A renowned pub with a welcoming ambiance, an extensive selection of craft beers on tap, and a secluded garden. It also features one of the finest courtyard terraces in the city, ivy-clad and with a fireplace.

10 Bar Le Saint-Sulpice
MAP L1 ■ 1680 Rue St-Denis
A well-known bar especially popular with partying university students. Contemporary music inside and a large garden make for an ideal night out.

See map on pp68–9

Downtown Restaurants

1 Otto Yakitori
MAP G1 ▪ 1441 Rue St-Mathieu ▪ (514) 507 8886 ▪ $

Specializing in grilled and skewered meat and vegetables, this charming Japanese pub stays open until late in the night.

2 Bouillon Bilk
MAP K2 ▪ 1595 Blvd St-Laurent ▪ (514) 845 1595 ▪ www.bouillon bilk.com ▪ $$$

The minimalist setting is a quiet contrast to the French-inspired creativity. Try the braised port with pea ravioli.

3 Le Café des Beaux-Arts
MAP C3 ▪ 1384 Rue Sherbrooke Ouest ▪ (514) 843 3233 ▪ www.mbam.qc.ca ▪ $$

Delicious French bistro cuisine awaits you inside the luxurious confines of the Musée des Beaux-Arts *(see pp24–5)*.

4 Les Enfants Terribles
MAP J2 ▪ 44th floor, 1 Place Ville-Marie ▪ www.jesuisunenfant terrible.com ▪ $$

Visit this bustling French brasserie for great food and a stunning view. Try the oysters and the bavette steak.

5 Maison Boulud
MAP J1 ▪ 1228 Rue Sherbrooke Ouest ▪ (514) 842 4224 ▪ www.maisonboulud.com ▪ $$$

Helmed by Chef Daniel Boulud, this grand restaurant features French-Québécois cuisine.

Glitzy dining at Maison Boulud

6 Cuisine Aunt Dai
MAP G1 ▪ 1448 Rue St-Mathieu ▪ (514) 935 1067 ▪ www.auntdai.com ▪ $

This Chinatown restaurant is popular with students for its affordable and tasty dishes. The online menu has notes from the owner on each dish.

7 Café Parvis
MAP J1 ▪ 433 Rue Mayor ▪ (514) 764 3589 ▪ www.cafe parvis.com ▪ $$

An oasis in the heart of downtown Montreal. Excellent for brunch, pizzas, and salads to share.

8 Ferreira Café
MAP J1 ▪ 1446 Rue Peel ▪ (514) 848 0988 ▪ www.ferreira cafe.com ▪ $$

Dig into dishes like grilled shrimp with garlic and brandy at this bustling restaurant run by the well-known Portuguese chef Carlos Ferreira.

9 Fiorellino
MAP J2 ▪ 470 Rue de la Gauchetiére O ▪ (514) 878 3666 ▪ www.fiorellino.ca ▪ $$

Come here for delicious, simple Italian cuisine. The wood-fired pizzas here draw a crowd, but the pasta and desserts are also superb.

10 La Habanera
MAP J2 ▪ 1216 Ave Union ▪ (514) 375 5355 ▪ www.lahabanera.ca ▪ $

Colorful Cuban café with small plates to share and excellent cocktails. Try their take on the classic poutine – it's made with yucca.

Quartier Latin Restaurants

PRICE CATEGORIES
For a three-course meal for one with half a bottle of wine (or equivalent meal), taxes and extra charges.

$ under $40 $$ $40–$80 $$$ over $80

1 Le Saloon
MAP M1 ■ 1333 Rue Ste-Catherine Est ■ (514) 522 1333 ■ www.lesaloon.ca ■ $$

This amiable bistro in the heart of Gay Village serves juicy burgers, hearty sandwiches, fresh salads, and fruity cocktails, along with nachos, poutine, and a lively weekend brunch.

2 La Chilentia
MAP D3 ■ 130 Rue Roy Est ■ (514) 286 6075 ■ www.lachilenita.com ■ $

Enjoy traditional Chilean and Mexican dishes at this small restaurant with a relaxed vibe. The empanadas are a good place to start

3 Mañana
MAP E3 ■ 3605 Rue St-Denis ■ (514) 847 1050 ■ $$

This Mexican restaurant offers an experience of the country, without falling into the usual clichés. The banana flambé with red wine and tequila is delicious.

4 Acajou Br
MAP E3 ■ 3425A Rue St-Denis ■ (514) 963 7064 ■ $$

Brazilian dishes such as *moqueca de poisson et crevette* (fish and shrimp stew) and *feijoada* (black bean stew) are served in a small, modern dining room, with exposed brick walls and contemporary decor.

5 Restaurant Tendresse
MAP M1 ■ 1259 Rue St-Catherine Est ■ (438) 387 1471 ■ $$

A trendy vegan restaurant that serves plant-based brunches, lunches, and dinners in a bright and airy space.

6 Le Café Cherrier
MAP E3 ■ 3635 Rue St-Denis ■ (514) 843 4308 ■ www.cafe cherrier.ca ■ $$

This French bistro has one of the best terraces in Montreal, which makes its weekend brunches quite a social event.

Le Café Cherrier

7 Uniburger
MAP L1 ■ 2001 Rue St-Denis ■ (514) 419 6555 ■ www.uniburger.com ■ $

Known for serving the best burgers in Montreal, this legendary, old-fashioned fast food joint is a must-try.

8 O'Thym
MAP M1 ■ 1112 Blvd de Maisonneuve (cnr Amherst) ■ (514) 525 3443 ■ www.othym.com ■ $$

This bring-your-own-wine bistro offers dishes based on local ingredients, including venison, salmon, and duck.

9 Le Passé Composé
MAP M1 ■ 1310 Blvd de Maisonneuve Est ■ (514) 524 6663 ■ www.bistropassecompose.com ■ $$

With a reasonably priced *table d'hôte*, this neighborhood French bistro opens for breakfast, lunch, and supper.

10 Café Saigon
MAP M1 ■ 1280 Rue St-André ■ (514) 849 0429 ■ $

Popular with the university crowd, this Asian BYO café is famous for its shrimp soup and spring rolls.

See map on pp68–9

TOP10 Mont-Royal to Hochelaga-Maisonneuve

This generous swath of Montreal includes the most prominent green space and some of the finest attractions of the entire city. The fertile, rolling expanse that makes up Parc du Mont-Royal spreads gracefully into the bustle below – with the city's most diverse areas such as Little Italy, Rosemont, and Mercier. Here you'll find shops, markets, and restaurants offering every imaginable temptation. For those favoring the outdoor life, the mountain provides an inviting backdrop for a wide range of activities. The Parc Olympique, including the Stade Olympique, Jardin Botanique, and Insectarium, provide visitors, young and old, with an array of entertainment.

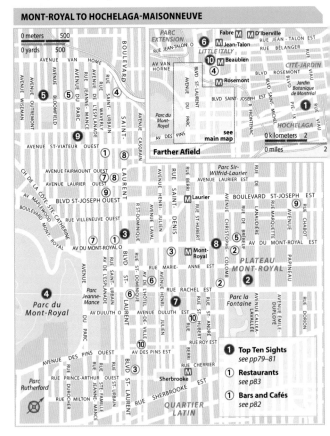

MONT-ROYAL TO HOCHELAGA-MAISONNEUVE

1 Top Ten Sights
see pp79–81

1 Restaurants
see p83

1 Bars and Cafés
see p82

The Olympic Stadium, the centerpiece of Parc Olympique

1 Parc Olympique

This astonishing attraction offers exhilarating activities for all age groups. From the dizzying heights of the world's highest leaning tower, the Tour Montréal atop the Stade Olympique, to the beautiful of the Jardin Botanique, not to mention the awe-inspiring journey through space at the Planétarium Rio Tinto Alcan – you can easily spend a full day or two exploring this area *(see pp18–21)*.

2 Le Plateau Mont-Royal
MAP E2

Plateau Mont-Royal begins at Rue Sherbrooke and Boulevard Saint-Laurent and spreads northward to Avenue Laurier and east to Parc Lafontaine. This architecturally rich neighborhood was made up of separate villages before being absorbed by the City of Montreal. Ornate duplexes abound on tree-lined streets, where you can see exterior staircases, wrought-iron banisters, and fine woodwork. The area is busy day and night with clubs, restaurants, shops, and markets.

3 Boulevard Saint-Laurent
MAP D2

East meets west at this long boulevard, referred to as "the Main." Beginning at the waterfront, it designates the symbolic dividing line between the Anglophone west side and the Francophone east side of the city, although in contemporary Montreal this division has all but vanished these days. Here you'll find designer boutiques, chic cafés and sushi bars, gourmet restaurants, and up-to-the-minute nightclubs sometimes stacked two and three floors high, underlining the street's international party reputation. You can buy almost anything you desire here, from cheap clothing to food, antiquarian books, high-tech equipment, diamonds, crafts, kitchenware – even gravestones.

Parc du Mont-Royal

4 Parc du Mont-Royal

Mont-Royal, after which Montreal is named, defines the city's personality with its year-round outdoor attractions, peaceful cemetery, and lush, rolling breadth above the St Lawrence River. Parc du Mont-Royal has the distinction of being the first place in Quebec to receive historic and natural heritage status, meaning it is protected as a green space *(see pp12–13)*.

Stalls piled high with fresh produce at the Marché Jean-Talon

⑤ Outremont
MAP C1

Founded in 1695, this area, meaning "beyond the mountain," is the predominantly French-speaking wealthy residential quarter. It features some of the most luxurious mansions in the city, and the main thoroughfares of Avenue Laurier and Rue Bernard west of Avenue du Parc are peppered with expensive fashion boutiques, exclusive hair salons, and hip eateries serving a clientele more akin to Paris than North America. Don't miss one of the country's finest *fromageries* (cheese-makers), Fromagerie Yannick (1218 Rue Bernard), or the rich pastries at Hof Kelsten (4524 Blvd St-Laurent). You can get lost in this area due to the meandering streets, so keep a mental note of your route.

⑥ Marché Jean-Talon
MAP P6 ▪ Métro Jean-Talon

A walk through the alluring Marché Jean-Talon tempts the senses with a profusion of fresh market fare, imported Italian gourmet luxuries, and homemade marvels from traditional local kitchens. Fresh produce is brought to market daily by dozens of farmers from outlying regions, together with discerning local importers. Also inside the market area is the Marché des Saveurs du Québec, a market within a market, which departs from the Italian theme and presents a line-up of specialties from Quebec Province.

> **MAISON DE LA CULTURE**
>
> Montreal has one of the most prized cultural networks in the world, evident in a system of venues called Maison de la Culture (house of culture) where music, art, and symposia are offered to the public for free or at minimal cost. The best example is the Chapelle Historique du Bon-Pasteur at 100 Rue Sherbrooke Est, which has now become a concert hall.

⑦ Rue Saint-Denis
MAP E2

Architectural treasures, street poets, clothing stores, and a plethora of restaurants and cafés are the main attractions on this street. From Old Montreal's Carré Viger north to Carré Saint-Louis, the Victorian architecture seems to blend effortlessly with the designer

Vibrant Rue Saint-Denis

stores, hip-hop music culture, and the buzzing youthful vitality that is the essence of this area.

8 Avenue du Mont-Royal
MAP D2

This street has vitality and panache, reflected in its bevy of eclectic eateries, curiosity shops, and cafés, but mostly in the laid-back attitude of its residents. Bargain shops nestle beside boutiques, while markets sell everything from fashion to food.

9 Avenue du Parc
MAP D2

Starting at Rue Sherbrooke heading north, this riotous thoroughfare slices through the principal neighborhoods of the city. You can spend a whole day on this one street alone: enjoying the Tam-Tam drum festival (Sundays only), sampling Greek, Lebanese or Italian cuisine, shopping for bargains or custom-made leather coats in the afternoon, then stopping for a swim at the YMCA, and finally enjoying a drink while listening to live African music.

Tam-Tam festival, Avenue du Parc

10 Little Italy
MAP P6 ■ Métro Jean-Talon

Italian Canadians make up Montreal's largest immigrant community and can trace their presence in the city back to the early 19th century. Today, Boulevard Saint-Laurent provides the Italian version of café society in a stream of cafés and restaurants, but Little Italy proper is defined by the borders of Rue Jean-Talon, Rue Saint-Zotique, Rue Marconi, and Avenue Drolet. Nudging up against Little Italy is the arty neighborhood of Mile-Ex.

A DAY'S WALK AROUND MONT-ROYAL

▶ MORNING

Take the No. 11 bus from Mont-Royal Métro station up Avenue du Mont-Royal and you will be able to see the **Parc Olympique** *(see pp18–21)* to the east. Disembark at **Lac aux Castors** *(see p13)* and walk around the lakeside trail to see resident ducks and geese. Follow the trail, veering to your left, to Chemin Olmsted, which leads you past sculptures of the International Sculpture Symposium. Continue to **Maison Smith** *(see p13)*, and take in the wonderful exhibit presented by **Les Amis de la Montagne** (Friends of the Mountain).

Return to Chemin Olmsted and follow the trail left to the commemorative Olmsted plaque embedded in rock, and then on to the main **chalet** and **Kondiaronk Lookout** *(see p12)*, the best viewpoint of the city. Return to the path behind the chalet, turn right and a little farther on, climb the path on your left to the foot of **La Croix** *(see p12)*, the most recognized symbol of Montreal.

Return to Maison Smith to take the bus back to Mont-Royal station, and then head to nearby Beautys *(93 av du Mont-Royal Ouest)*, a beloved 1950s diner – try the bagel with eggs, bacon, and cheese. Then stroll east on buzzing **Avenue du Mont-Royal**.

AFTERNOON

You can either spend the afternoon enjoying some of the best shopping in the area on Avenue Duluth, or relax in the lovely **Parc Lafontaine** *(see p46)*.

See map on p78 ←

Bars and Cafés

1 Café Olimpico
MAP D1
■ 124 Rue St-Viateur Ouest

Founded in 1970, this phenomenally popular Italian café in the uber-hip Mile End district is packed with regulars who swear that its lattes are the city's best.

Café Olimpico

2 Barraca Rhumerie et Tapas
MAP E2 ■ 1134 Ave du Mont-Royal Est

This tightly packed spot is popular with young people who have a penchant for rum. Dozens of brands from 11 countries are served alongside delicious tapas.

3 Bílý Kůň
MAP E2
■ 354 Ave du Mont-Royal Est

Busy Czech microbrewery with live jazz, classical performances, and DJs. Good bar snacks too.

4 Isle De Garde
MAP E1
■ 1039 Rue Beaubien Est

This cozy bar pours an innovative array of beer, from Berliner Melon Weisse (from Dunham, Quebec) to dry, tart ciders, and the house-made Isle de Garde Brown Porter ale.

5 Café Rico
MAP E2 ■ 1215 Ave du Mont-Royal Est

Established in 1998, this friendly café and bean roaster serves organic and certified fair-trade coffee, along with fresh pastries and sandwiches.

6 Café Néve
MAP D2 ■ 151 Rue Rachel Est

This is the flagship location of the artisanal coffee chain founded in Montreal. It offers coffee lovers a wonderful ambiance to go with its famous cookies. Brunch is served until 2pm every day, and includes eggs benedict, *croque monsieur*, and various tartines.

7 Bar Henrietta
MAP D1 ■ 115 Ave Laurier Ouest

Enjoy Portuguese-tavern-inspired food at this bustling restaurant. There is also an extensive cocktail and wine list.

8 Sparrow
MAP D1 ■ 5322 Blvd St-Laurent

With an eclectic background music selection, this casual cocktail bar has a warm and vintage feel to it. Try their weekend brunch, which pairs well with the excellent beers on tap.

9 Roseline
MAP D1 ■ 5014 Blvd Saint-Laurent ■ (514) 544 6869

A wine bar with a prohibition kind of vibe and an incredible menu of French cuisine. Try the Duck Magret and Baked Alaska.

10 Else's
MAP E2 ■ 156 Rue Roy Est

This favored neighborhood bar for musicians, artists, and other creatives serves a homey menu of juicy burgers, sausages, shrimp tacos, and signature breads.

Restaurants

1 Beauty's
MAP D2 ▪ 93 Ave du Mont-Royal Ouest ▪ (514) 849 8883 ▪ $

Opened in 1942, this diner is a local favorite. Try the "Beauty's special" breakfast here, along with a smoothie.

2 Ty-Breiz Crêperie Bretonne
MAP E2 ▪ 933 Rue Rachel Est ▪ (514) 521 1444 ▪ $

Step into this perennial favorite and taste Bretonne food in its traditional forms, from onion soup and frog's legs to the assortment of crêpes.

3 Maestro SVP
MAP D2 ▪ 3615 Blvd St-Laurent ▪ (514) 842 6447 ▪ $$

This is the place for oysters. Try them fresh, baked, or in a shooter with vodka and horseradish sauce.

4 Le Butterblume
MAP D1 ▪ 5836 Blvd Saint-Laurent ▪ (514) 903 9115 ▪ $$

The restaurant is charming, the bread homemade, and the food – such as Atlantic salmon blinis and red quinoa salad – is delicious.

5 Lester's Deli
MAP D2 ▪ 1057 Ave Bernard ▪ (514) 213 1313 ▪ $

Founded in 1951, this family-run deli is known for its smoked meat

sandwiches, and the owner's witty banter. Look out for his mustard bottle prank.

6 Patati Patata Friterie Deluxe
MAP D2 ▪ 4177 Blvd St-Laurent ▪ (514) 844 0216 ▪ $

A little, budget-friendly burger joint that also serves a classic poutine, crêpes, and fresh juices.

7 Le Filet
MAP D2 ▪ 219 Ave du Mont-Royal Ouest ▪ (514) 360 6060 ▪ $$

At this sleek seafood restaurant the fresh fish and shellfish shine, with minimal but well-selected garnishes.

8 Wilensky's Light Lunch
MAP D1 ▪ 34 Ave Fairmont Ouest ▪ (514) 271 0247 ▪ Closed Sun ▪ $

Deli serving egg cream sodas and grilled salami, bologna, and Swiss-cheese sandwiches since 1932.

9 Le Pégase
1831 Rue Gilford ▪ (514) 522 0487 ▪ $$

Bring your own wine to complement the French food at this small bistro.

10 Au Pied De Cochon
MAP E2 ▪ 536 Ave Duluth Est ▪ (514) 281 1114 ▪ $$

A meat-centric restaurant where the chef, Martin Picard, has a playful approach to Québécois cuisine.

Diners at the popular Lester's Deli

See map on p78 ←

⒑⁰ᵖ Excursions from Montreal

On Friday nights and Saturday mornings Montreal's bridges are crowded with residents traveling out of town to enjoy the activities possible in the surrounding countryside. Les Laurentides (the Laurentian mountains) and the Cantons-de-l'Est (the Eastern Townships) are where Montrealers venture to hike in summer or ski in winter. Traffic through the locks at Sainte-Anne-de-Bellevue also buzzes with boaters heading west on the Ottawa River or east to Trois-Rivières, Quebec City, and on to the Atlantic Ocean. Beaches at Parc National d'Oka, Lac Memphrémagog, or Lac des Sables draw sun-lovers in summer.

Caribou, Parc Oméga, Outaouais

EXCURSIONS FROM MONTREAL

Mont Tremblant village buried in the Laurentian mountains

1 Les Laurentides

Only an hour from the congestion of Montreal, the stunning Laurentian mountains north of the city provide an astounding list of activities. In summer there are endless opportunities to swim, fish, raft, horse-ride, play golf, mountain climb, or just relax in the sunny rural setting. Winter brings the chance to ski (downhill or cross-country), go tobogganing or snowboarding *(see pp36–7)*.

2 Outaouais

MAP N5 ■ Oméga Park: 399 Rte 323 N ■ Manoir Louis-Joseph-Papineau: 500 Rue Notre-Dame, Montebello; open May & Jun: 10am–5pm Fri & Sat, Jul & Aug: 10am–5pm daily, Sep & Oct: 10am–5pm Fri–Sun; Adm

This historic area west of Montreal was not settled by white people until the early 19th century, and it remains largely undeveloped. Don't miss Oméga Safari Park, just outside Montebello, with its 1,500 acres (607 ha) inhabited by roaming bison, wapitis, black bear, and wolves, then continue on to the Parc National de Plaisance along the Ottawa River, to see flocks of Canada geese. In Montebello itself visit Manoir Louis-Joseph-Papineau, a 19th-century home filled with antiques and local artifacts.

3 Hudson and Rigaud

MAP N6

A favorite jaunt west from Montreal, the communities of Hudson and Rigaud hug the mountains along the pastoral Ottawa River. Hudson, with its history of British settlement and fur trading, has historic mansions set on magnificent estates and an abundance of antiques shops, art galleries, and cafés. Its landscape is popular for equestrians, while its riverside setting draws a sailing crowd. The village of Rigaud is more French, maintaining its Gallic legacy in churches and family-run farms.

Cantons-de-l'Est (map)

Granby ① ④ ⑨ ⑨
Waterloo Sherbrooke
⑦ Bromont ② North
⑩ ③ Magog ② Hatley
⑥ ⑧ ⑧
⑤ Knowlton ⑤ ⑦ ⑧ ⑩
Brome ⑤ Coaticook
km 10 ④
miles 10 ② ⑥

(second map)

Princeville Thetford
Deschaillons-sur-Saint-Laurent Mines
Victoriaville La
Chesterville Guadeloupe
Saint-Joseph-
Warwick de-Coleraine
Beaulac Stornoway
Richmond
Dudswell Gould Laval-Nord
Scotstown ⑩
Sherbrooke ⑨③
La Patrie
Saint-Isidore-
de-Clifton
Magog NEW
Compton MAINE
HAMPSHIRE
Coaticook 0 km 25
VERMONT 0 miles 25

BRIDGES OF MONTREAL

Getting on and off the island city of Montreal can be daunting. Pay due respect to the French *"pont"* (bridge) signage, because once you are on a bridge, you must continue across it before you can turn around. There are a total of 18 bridges and one tunnel providing access to the city.

Deux-Montagnes
MAP N6 ■ www.ville.deux-montagnes.qc.ca

This community, 30 minutes' drive from Montreal, was first settled by the Sulpician Order during the French Regime, and the fresh produce of this region, including the famous Oka cheese, is a carry-over from the agricultural traditions begun by the priests. Parc National d'Oka offers camping, kayaking, hiking, and a sandy beach.

1000 Islands
Rte No. 401 ■ Boat trips: St Lawrence Cruise Lines: 1-800 267 7868 ■ www.stlawrencerivercruise.com

These islands are a great escape, accessible either by car or train to Brockville. About 2 hours west of the border of Ontario and Quebec, 1000 Islands actually covers 1,865 islands running the 50-mile (80-km) span from Brockville to Kingston, and were formed by metamorphic rock at the end of the last Ice Age. Thousand Islands National Park is the *pièce de résistance* with 21 main islands, most of which have camping facilities.

Bonaventure Island, 1000 Islands

Lanaudière
MAP P5 ■ www.lanaudiere.ca

From the St Lawrence River Valley rising to the Laurentian lowland plateau, there's a multitude of forests, lakes, rivers, and farmland to explore in this region, all within a few hours of Montreal. You can enjoy numerous activities here, indoors and out. The Festival de Lanaudière, Canada's most renowned classical music festival, takes place from early June to early August, with concerts staged at outdoor venues and heritage churches in Joliette.

Waterfall, Lanaudière

Montérégie
MAP P5 ■ Fort Chambly: 2 Rue Richelieu, Chambly ■ Open May–Oct: 10am–5pm Wed–Sun (Jun–Sep: daily; Jul–Aug: to 6pm) ■ Adm ■ www.tourisme-monteregie.qc.ca

To reach this huge region of plains, forests, and history, drive across the Pont Champlain, following signs for highway 10 eastward. Then take highway 133 (also called Chemin des Patriotes after the soldiers who fought the British here in 1837) toward Sorel, one of the oldest cities in Canada. Boat trips are possible around the town's many islands. Of major note in the region, which is known for its apple orchards and cider-making, is Fort Chambly. This well-preserved 18th-century fortress was built to defend the French from both Dutch and British attack.

Trois-Rivières
MAP Q5

Sieur de Laviolette founded this community in 1634, but the beautiful French Regime architecture that once graced the streets was ravaged by a monstrous fire that swept through the entire town in 1908. Only remnants of the original wall survive. Today the town is known as one of the main providers of pulp and paper in the world. Dominating the landscape is the Pôle Culturel du Monastère des Ursulines, a lovely church built by Ursuline nuns, surrounded by a public park. There are a plethora of cafés, bistros, and restaurants on Rue des Forges.

⑨ Parc National du Canada de la Mauricie

MAP P4 ■ Adm ■ www.pc.gc.ca

One of Canada's most spectacular areas of rivers, lakes, mountains, and wildlife, La Mauricie National Park is only a two-hour drive from downtown Montreal or Quebec City. It is accessible all year round, and is a perennial favorite with campers and outdoor enthusiasts. It is particularly popular with anglers, with trout and pike found in abundance in Lac Wapizagonke.

Canoeing, La Mauricie National Park

⑩ Cantons-de-l'Est

MAP Q6 ■ www.cantonsde lest.com

This natural wonderland is bounded by the Richelieu and St Lawrence rivers and the US states of Vermont, New Hampshire, and Maine. The biggest feature is the Appalachian Mountains, with top-notch hiking trails at Owl's Head, Mont Sutton, Mont Bromont, and Mont Orford. The villages of this vast district, such as Knowlton, are a remnant of 19th- century British settlement, their Victorian buildings now home to antiques shops and cafés *(see pp88–9).*

A DAY IN VAL-DAVID AND THE P'TIT TRAIN DU NORD TRAIL

▶ MORNING

Take Route 15, the Laurentian Autoroute, north to Exit 76, then join Route 117 north to the village of **Val-David** *(see p37)*. At the Municipalité de Val-David *(2501 Rue de l'Église)* you can obtain a map and detailed information about the region.

Walk down **Rue de l'Église** to visit the **1001 Pots Gallery and Gift Shop** *(2435 Rue de l'Église)*. This exhibition of handmade pottery and works of art is one of the largest ceramic shows in North America, produced by an esteemed collective of over 50 Québécois artists. For a great lunch, backtrack to Rue de la Sapinière and turn left to **C'est La Vie Café** *(1347 Rue de la Sapinière; (819) 320 0273)*.

AFTERNOON

After lunch, explore the **Parc Linéaire Le P'tit Train du Nord** *(see p48)*, a green swath of protected trails snaking 144 miles (232 km) through the Laurentides on the old mountain train path. The defunct railroad line is perfect for hiking, cycling, and walking in summer and cross-country skiing in winter. If cycling is your preference, Roc 'n' Ride *(2444 Rue de l'Église)* rents bikes.

Return to Val-David and, if you have the energy, shop for unusual Christmas decorations at **Village du Père Noël** *(987 Rue Morin)*, open all year. Then enjoy a Québécois dinner at **Restaurant au Petit Poucet** *(see p91)*.

See map on pp84–5

Attractions in Cantons-de-l'Est

1 Zoo de Granby
MAP Q6 ■ 1050 Blvd David-Bouchard, Granby ■ Opening times vary, check website ■ Adm ■ www.zoodegranby.com for details

This zoo is home to over 225 species of animals from around the globe.

2 Parc National du Mont-Orford
MAP Q6 ■ 3321 Chemin du Parc, Canton d'Orford

Rising majestically beside the Eastern Townships Autoroute, Mont Orford is the central area for outdoor activities in this sprawling preserve, covering over 22 sq miles (57 sq km) around the mountain.

3 Knowlton
MAP Q6

Set on the inviting shores of Lac Brome, this 19th-century Anglophone village has an idyllic locale, attracting vacationers.

4 Lac Memphrémagog
MAP Q6

This huge lake is a draw for boat-lovers. Legend has it that the lake is home to a "memphre" – a long-necked, dark green reptilian monster that has apparently been sighted over 200 times since 1847.

5 L'Abbaye de Saint-Benoît-du-Lac
MAP Q6 ■ Saint-Benoît-du-Lac ■ Open 5am–9pm daily

Benedictine monks founded this monastery overlooking Lac Memphrémagog in 1912. Gregorian chants take place daily at 7:30am, 11am, and 5pm.

6 Le Chemin des Vignobles de l'Estrie
MAP P6

Due to its slate soil and climate this area has a highly respected wine-growing tradition visible along the Wine Route (Hwy 202) between Dunham and Stanbridge East.

7 Frelighsburg
MAP P6

A peaceful town at the foot of Mount Pinnacle and near the US border, Frelighsburg's landscape attracts artists and photographers.

Fall landscape around Frelighsburg

8 Bromont
MAP Q6 ■ Le Musée de Chocolat: 679 Rue Shefford; 9am–5pm daily

Bromont embodies all the best of Cantons-de-l'Est: A charming main street is lined with antique shops and galleries; cozy restaurants serve farm-fresh cuisine; and the town is surrounded by the great outdoors. For a sweet visit stop into the Musée du Chocolat, where you can learn about chocolate-making while nibbling on fine specimens.

9 Sherbrooke
MAP Q6

The Rivière Saint-François bisects this commercial center of Cantons-de-l'Est. Despite its history of British settlement, today it is predominantly a French-speaking town.

10 Parc de la Gorge de Coaticook
MAP Q6

This park is set around a 165-ft (50-m) gorge, and offers hiking trails and horse riding, as well snow and ice activities in winter (see p90).

Restaurants in Cantons-de-l'Est

PRICE CATEGORIES

For a three-course meal for one with half
a bottle of wine (or equivalent meal),
taxes and extra charges

$ under $40 $$ $40–$80 $$$ over $80

1 Restaurant da Leonardo

MAP Q6 ■ 4664 Blvd Bourque,
Sherbrooke ■ (819) 564 0666 ■ $$

An upscale restaurant, Leonardo
opened in 1997 and serves traditional
Italian cuisine and excellent wine.
During summers, you can sit outside
on the sunny terrace.

2 Comme Chez Soi

MAP Q6 ■ 3219 Rue Principale
Ouest, Magog ■ (819) 868 2233 ■ $$

A table d'hôte restaurant, where
the set menu changes regularly.
Specialties include duck confit,
rack of lamb, and steak.

3 Auberge aux Toits Rouges

MAP off Q6 ■ 72 Rue Chesham,
Notre-Dame-des-Bois ■ (819) 888
2999 ■ $$

Located in the beautiful village of
Notre-Dame-des-Bois, this country
inn offers a menu of traditional
Mediterranean dishes. A must-try
is the *filet mignon*.

4 Siboire

MAP Q6 ■ 80 Rue du Dépôt,
Sherbrooke ■ (819) 565 3636 ■ $

Set in a former train station,
this spacious microbrewery is
known for its excellent fish and
chips. The adjoining terrace is
lovely on warmer days.

5 Auberge West Brome

MAP Q6 ■ 128 Rte 139, West
Brome ■ (888) 902 7663 ■ $$$

Luxurious Auberge West Brome
offers Lac Brome duck and other
regional specialties, grown in the
on-site organic vegetable garden, as
well as first-class accommodations.

6 L'Oeufrier

MAP Q6 ■ 109 Blvd du
Carrefour, Bromont ■ (450) 534
4494 ■ Closed Mon & Tue ■ $$

A gourmet restaurant, *chocolaterie*,
and auberge specializing in creative
dishes, ending with chocolate.

7 Le Cellier Du Roi Par Jérôme Ferrer

MAP Q6 ■ Le Royal Bromont, 400
Chemin Compton ■ (450) 534 4653
■ $$$

Amid the grounds of Le Royal Bromont
golf course, Chef Jérôme Ferrer showcases his Quebec-inspired cuisine with
a menu deeply rooted in the region.

Le Cellier Du Roi Par Jérôme Ferrer

8 Pinocchio

MAP Q6 ■ 469 Rue Principale
Ouest, Magog ■ (819) 868 8808 ■ $$

This chic, white-linen restaurant
offers fresh meat and seafood
dishes. The wine list is excellent.

9 La Table du Chef

MAP Q6 ■ 11 Rue Victoria,
Sherbrooke ■ (819) 562 2258 ■ $$

Run by renowned chef Alain
Labrie, this stylish restaurant excels
at French-accented regional cuisine,
including grilled bison and wild boar.

10 Auberge du Joli Vent

MAP Q6 ■ 667 Chemin
Bondville, Lac-Brome ■ (450) 243 4272
■ Open Fri & Sat D only (Jul–Aug Thu
also) ■ $$

A weekly changing menu features
innovative dishes using locally
sourced seasonal ingredients.

See map on pp84–5

Natural Sights

① Missisquoi Bay
MAP P6

The traditional home of the Abenaki people, this lush area in the western corner of Cantons-de-l'Est was the first refuge for Loyalist settlers crossing into Canada after the American Revolution.

② The Orchards
MAP Q6

The best territory for apples in the province is the Montérégie Region, but Cantons-de-l'Est also has plenty of orchards around Dunham, Brigham, Compton, and Stanbridge.

③ Lac Brome
MAP Q6

Lac Brome has several delightful lakeside communities: Knowlton, Foster, Bondville, Fulford, Iron Hill, East Hill, and West Brome – all retain in part a bygone way of life.

④ Route Saint-Armand
MAP Q6

In 1748 the Seigneurie Saint-Armand was given to René-Nicholas Levasseur by the King of France. Much of this grand property can be seen today on the roads from Vale Perkins on Lac Memphrémagog to Saint-Armand.

⑤ Mont Sutton
MAP Q6

Since it opened in 1960, Mont Sutton has been a favorite with downhill skiers due to its superior slopes.

⑥ Mont Owl's Head
MAP Q6

Set above Lac Memphrémagog, this ski resort has a vertical drop of 1,770 ft (540 m). An annual autumn music festival is held at the end of September.

⑦ Lac Massawippi
MAP Q6

Celebrities on the list of regulars at the Manoir Hovey resort here (see p113). Le Festival du Lac Massawippi runs popular music concerts from June until the end of August.

⑧ Parc de la Gorge de Coaticook
MAP Q6

Over 50,000 years ago the Wisconsin Glacier started to melt, giving birth to the Coaticook Lake and then this river, which dug a cavernous gorge. It now attracts visitors to the longest pedestrian suspension bridge in North America (see p88).

⑨ Parc National du Mont-Mégantic
Rte No. 257

Stargazing is the rule in this huge natural wonderland as the Astrolab beckons astronomers of every level.

⑩ Lac Mégantic
Rte No. 161

Located at the eastern edge of the townships in the Appalachian foothills, this peaceful lake provides outdoor activities and has a beach.

Riding the chairlift to the top of Mont Sutton

Local and Québécois Cuisine

PRICE CATEGORIES

For a three-course meal for one with half a bottle of wine (or equivalent meal), taxes and extra charges.

$ under $40 ■ $$ $40–$80 ■ $$$ over $80

1 Cap Saint-Jacques Maison de la Ferme Ecologique

MAP N6 ■ 183 Chemin du Cap-Saint-Jacques, Pierrefonds ■ (514) 280 6871 ■ Closed D ■ $

Visit this large organic farm and meet the chickens, taste the local maple syrup and honey, and pick up fresh vegetables and preserves from the on-site store.

2 Owl's Bread Bakery

MAP Q6 ■ 299A Rue Principale, Mansonville ■ (450) 292 3088 ■ $

This artisanal French bakery is also a high-end grocery and bistro. Almost all ingredients are organic and local.

3 Sucrerie de la Montagne

MAP N6 ■ 300 Chemin St Georges, Rigaud ■ (450) 451 0831 ■ $$

Pierre Faucher's maple sugar house serves Québécois cuisine such as pea soup, *tourtière* (meat pie), wood-fired baked beans, maple-glazed smoked ham, and maple sugar pie.

4 C'est la Vie

MAP N5 ■ 708 Rue de St-Jovite, Mont-Tremblant ■ (819) 681 0779 ■ $$$

An upscale restaurant serving French- and Québécois-inspired dishes; those made on the hot stone are highly recommended. The menu has plenty of gluten-free options too.

5 Le Lupin

MAP Q5 ■ 376 Rue St-Georges, Trois-Rivières ■ (819) 370 4740 ■ $$

An inviting "bring your own bottle" restaurant serving home-style local dishes, from sweet and savoury crepes to mussels and steaks.

6 Ferme Apicole Intermiel

MAP N5 ■ 10291 rang de la Fresnière, Mirabel ■ (450) 258 2713 ■ Closed D ■ $

This farm offers wonderful picnic sites with an abundance of apiary products to taste afterwards, such as honey mead and honey cookies.

Honey bees, Ferme Apicole Intermiel

7 Restaurant au Petit Poucet

MAP N5 ■ 1030 Rte 117, Val David ■ (819) 322 2246 ■ $$

Find mouth-watering, maple-smoked ham, meat pies, and sugar pies at this rustic cottage established in 1945.

8 Poivre Noir

MAP Q5 ■ 1300 Rue du Fleuve, Trois-Rivières ■ (819) 378 5772 ■ $$$

Dig into dishes crafted in Québécois style, from bison tartare to rich foie gras with smoked apple.

9 Le Petite Cachée

MAP N5 ■ 2681 Chemin du Village, Mont Tremblant ■ (819) 425 2654 ■ $$$

Known for its traditional French and Québécois cuisine, Le Petite Cachée is a charming bistro. Try the braised beef ribs or the pan-seared Arctic char.

10 Restaurant L'Imperial

MAP Q6 ■ 320 Blvd Leclerc, Local 28, Granby ■ (450) 994 1922 ■ Closed Mon ■ $$$

Run by renowned chef Jean-Philippe Tastet, this destination restaurant serves tasty duck bolognese ravioli, pistachio-stuffed rabbit, and indulgent desserts. Extensive wine list.

See map on pp84–5

📟 Quebec City

Shop at Petit-Champlain

Europeans first settled here in 1608, and throughout its history Quebec City has been the focus of political struggle between the British and the French – a battle that still rages today in this home of French separatism. Yet despite this turmoil, with its beautiful riverside setting, heritage sites, and cobblestone streets – all of which earned it World Heritage status in 1985 – the city is a traveler's dream. Poised upon the Cap Diamant escarpment overlooking the St Lawrence River and Les Laurentides, the city is home to a Francophone population rich in cultural pride and exuberance, magnificent architecture, preserved churches and monuments, fine cuisine, and numerous opportunities for outdoor adventure.

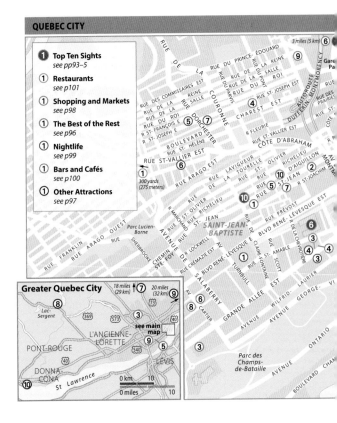

QUEBEC CITY

1. **Top Ten Sights**
   see pp93–5
2. **Restaurants**
   see p101
3. **Shopping and Markets**
   see p98
4. **The Best of the Rest**
   see p96
5. **Nightlife**
   see p99
6. **Bars and Cafés**
   see p100
7. **Other Attractions**
   see p97

Greater Quebec City

Aerial view, La Citadelle

① La Citadelle

Strategically perched on the precipice of Cap Diamant with a full 360-degree view, this powerful bastion would daunt the bravest of enemies approaching the riverside city. All you need to do is attend one of its summertime cannon-firing demonstrations to appreciate the persuasive power of this mighty fortress (see pp28–9).

② Musée de la Civilisation de Québec

Architect Moishe Safdie mirrored the surrounding neighborhood by incorporating the French Regime style in his design for this interesting building. Inside, however, it is another story – a futuristic world complete with a range of interactive exhibitions, as well as displays of folk art, religious icons, antique furniture in period settings, and everyday items that illustrate life in the city during its 400-year his-tory. There are also collaborative exhibitions at the Musée de l'Amérique Francophone (currently closed for renovations and set to reopen in 2024) (see pp30–31).

③ Château Frontenac

The most photographed landmark in the city, this hotel with its green copper roof is an architectural jewel designed by architect Bruce Price as a French-style château. Since it opened in 1893, the hotel has welcomed the rich, the famous, and the noble through its doors and into its plush salons. Guided tours are available (see p112).

The imposing Château Frontenac

TROMPE-L'OEIL

Trompe-l'oeil means "to deceive the eye" and if you are in the Quartier Saint-Roch district of Quebec City (near the train station) you can see a marvelous example of this art tradition on the columns on Rue Charest Est. Combining the energetic talents of street graffiti artists under the guidance of a trained painter, a project evolved creating *trompe l'oeil* paintings to decorate cement highway pillars. The results are astounding and have led to the graffiti artists forming their own legitimate company.

 Quartier Petit-Champlain

MAP M5

Home to 17th-century artisans and dockworkers in the 19th century, the houses in this area have now been renovated and adapted into an attractive range of eclectic gift shops, transforming what is the oldest part of the city into today's liveliest quarter. Maple butter, French macramé, and sculpted cherrywood cribs are just a few of the many unusual treats you can purchase here. Along the way you can eat and drink in the bars and cafés lining the pedestrianized streets.

 Parc des Champs-de-Bataille

MAP K6 ■ Open 9am–5:30pm daily ■ Adm

Designed to commemorate both French and British soldiers, the Plains of Abraham Museum is located within one of the park's many historic buildings and offers an inventive agenda to illustrate one of North America's most historic sites. The highlight is a multimedia show recounting the battles of 1759 and 1760 that took place here, and which led to a French defeat by the British *(see p40)*. An imposing mural by Quebec artist Aline Martineau depicts the establishment of the park in the 1930s and how it has changed over the years *(see p47)*.

 Observatoire de la capitale

MAP J6 ■ 1037 Rue de la Chevrotière ■ Open 10am–5pm daily (closed mid-Oct–Jan: Mon) ■ Adm

From the 31st floor of the Capital Observatory you can enjoy marvelous views of the entire area. Adding to the experience are the taped interpretation guides offering interesting information about the city in French, English, and Spanish. You can also learn about many aspects of the city's history at the interactive Horizons exhibit. Many city tours begin or end here too.

 Place Royale

MAP M5

The site of Nouvelle-France's first settlement, built by Samuel de Champlain in 1608, has been the hub of the city's cultural activities throughout its history. Shipbuilders, merchants, clergy, and everyday citizens once gathered here to conduct commerce, celebrate harvests, marry, drink, and bury their dead. Today, festivals such as Les Fêtes de la Nouvelle-France *(see p57)* rekindle the days of the early settlers with theatrical performances and traditional music. Don't miss Église Notre-Dame-des-Victoires, which has a collection of paintings by Van Dyck depicting the French victory over the British in 1690 *(see p31)*.

Notre-Dame-des-Victoires, Place Royale

8 Place de l'Hôtel de Ville
MAP L5

In the 18th century this square was the site of the Notre-Dame market and is still a popular gathering place for locals. During the summer it is often jammed with visitors who come to enjoy free music concerts and performances by local actors. The Romanesque architecture, as seen in the Hôtel de Ville (town hall) immediately beside the square, lends the area an imposing air.

Place de l'Hôtel de Ville

9 Le Grand Marché de Québec
MAP P3 ■ 250 Blvd Wilfrid-Hamel ■ (418) 692 2517

The city's first covered markets were built in the early 19th century at the main public squares. Le Grand Marché de Québec was built in 2021, echoing the traditional farmers' markets of the past. This new area is large and well-lit, with numerous restaurants, family spaces, and stalls tempting chefs with fresh produce.

10 Faubourg Saint-Jean-Baptiste
MAP H5

Built as a military defence against the British in the 18th century, the striking stone gate (Porte Saint-Jean) is the starting point for a popular 3-mile (4-km) walk along the city's ramparts. The area around the gate, also known as Quartier Montcalm, has a concentration of Québécois specialty merchants, as well as designer boutiques, cultural outlets, and nightclubs. This zone is famous for its bistros and restaurants serving fine French cuisine.

A DAY EXPLORING THE OLD TOWN

▶ MORNING

Start your day at **Château Frontenac** *(see p93)* for a breathtaking view of the St Lawrence River, Basse-Ville, Vieux-Port, and Île d'Orléans *(see pp34–5)* in the distance. Immediately beside the hotel runs **Terrasse-Dufferin** *(see p97)*, a boardwalk clinging to the rock escarpment complete with ornate Parisian-style street lamps. After taking in the exhilarating surroundings, stroll through the **Jardins des Gouverneurs** and look for monuments to Wolfe and Montcalm, the French and English generals in the Battle of the Plains of Abraham *(see p40)*.

Go back along Terrasse-Dufferin to **Quartier Petit-Champlain**, the oldest merchant district in North America, with its dazzling variety of boutiques and souvenir shops.

Enjoy hearty local fare, like rabbit lasagne and cheese fondue, at the inviting **Lapin Sauté** *(52 Rue du Petit-Champlain)*.

AFTERNOON

If you want to stretch your legs after lunch, follow the natural flow of the land to the waterfront, head left along **Rue Dalhousie** and the Vieux-Port, and turn left at **Rue St-André**. Here you'll find inspiring public art, tempting restaurants, and cool bike rental shops. Hire a bike and explore the area at your leisure.

For an early evening cocktail and, perhaps, a bite of something fresh and local, head over to **Chez Rioux & Pettigrew** *(160 Rue St-Paul)*.

See map on pp92–3 ←

The Best of the Rest

1 Place D'Youville
MAP K5

This popular square, located in front of the 18th-century stone gate Porte Saint-Jean, bustles with activity. Outdoor music concerts are held here in summer and there is an ice-skating rink from October to March.

2 Maison de la Littérature
MAP L5 ▪ 40 Rue St-Stanislas ▪ (418) 641 6797

Housed in a former Methodist church, this beautiful public library is dedicated to the preservation of the French language.

3 Musée National des Beaux-Arts du Québec
MAP K6 ▪ 179 Grande Allée Ouest ▪ Open 10am–5pm Tue–Sun (to 9pm Wed) ▪ Adm

These four distinct pavilions (including a former jailhouse) exhibit works by Québécois and international artists.

4 Morrin Centre
MAP L5 ▪ 44 Chaussée des Écossais ▪ Open noon–4pm Wed–Sun & noon–8pm Tue ▪ Adm

Historic site with guided tours taking you through 18th-century prisons.

Quebec City to Lévis Ferry

5 Quebec City to Lévis Ferry
MAP M5 ▪ 10 Rue des Traversiers

This 10-minute crossing offers a stunning view of the city.

Porte Saint-Louis

6 Porte Saint-Louis
MAP K5

Although constructed to defend the city in the 18th century, the city walls were an impediment to commerce. Eventually, gates such as Porte Saint-Louis had to be cut into the fortifications.

7 L'Îlot des Palais
MAP K4 ▪ 8 Rue Valliére ▪ Open Jan–May: 1–4:30pm Thu & Fri, 10am–5pm Sat & Sun; Jun & Oct: 10am–5pm Tue–Sun (Jul–early Sep: daily) ▪ Adm

Quebec City's history is interpreted in a number of interactive displays.

8 Hôtel du Parlement
MAP K5 ▪ 1045 Rue des Parlementaires ▪ Open Sep–Jun: 8am–5pm Mon–Fri; Jun–Sep: 8:30am–4:30pm Mon–Fri, 9:30am–4:30pm Sat & Sun

The city's political forum is housed in this imposing structure.

9 Monastère des Augustines
MAP K4 ▪ 77 Rue des Remparts ▪ www.monastere.ca

Once a monastery for the Augustine sisters, it is now a health and wellness retreat, restaurant, and museum.

10 Pôle Culturel du Monastère des Ursulines
MAP L5 ▪ 12 Rue Donnaconna ▪ Open 10am–5pm Tue–Sun (from 1pm Oct–Apr) ▪ Adm

Housed in a 17th-century convent, exhibits tell the story of the first school for girls established here.

Other Attractions

1 Musée du Fort
MAP L5 ▪ 10 Rue Ste-Anne
▪ Open Apr–Oct: 10am–5pm daily;
Nov, Feb–Mar: 11am–4pm Thu–Sun
▪ Adm

State-of-the-art technology has
created a diorama that illustrates
the tale of this walled city.

2 Terrasse Pierre-Dugua-de-Mons
MAP L5 ▪ End of Rue de la Porte

Come here for incredible views of Île
d'Orléans, the St Lawrence River, the
South Shore, and Mont Sainte-Anne.

3 Parc de l'Artillerie
MAP K4 ▪ 2 Rue d'Auteuil
▪ Open May–Oct: 10am–5pm daily
▪ Adm

Tour 17th- and 18th-century defensive
buildings, including an ammunition
factory used until the 1960s.

4 Les Glissades de la Terrasse-Dufferin
MAP L5 ▪ Open mid-Dec–mid-Mar:
10am–5pm daily (to 9pm Fri & Sat)
▪ Adm

This winter attraction features three
icy toboggan runs bolting participants
down a steep 820-ft (250-m) incline.

5 Galerie d'art Inuit Brousseau
MAP L5 ▪ 35 Rue St-Louis
▪ Open 9:30am–5:30pm
daily ▪ www.artinuit.ca

The Inuit sculptures
displayed here illustrate
the lifestyles and tradi-
tions of these Indigenous
Canadian peoples.

6 Boutique Métiers d'Art du Québec
MAP M5 ▪ 29 Rue
Notre-Dame ▪ Open
10am–5pm daily

**Sculpture, Musée
d'art Inuit Brousseau**

Craft gallery dedicated to selling
only locally produced works of art
including hand-blown glass objects.

7 Parc National de la Jacques-Cartier
MAP P2 ▪ 103 Chemin du
Parc-National

Located 28 miles (45 km) from
downtown Quebec City, this immense
park abounds with lakes, mountains,
and outdoor activities in all seasons.

Parc National de la Jacques-Cartier

8 Station Touristique Duchesnay
MAP N3 ▪ 140 Montée de l'Auberge,
Sainte Catherine de la Jacques Cartier

To see the glorious Canadian forests,
head west toward Sainte-Catherine-
de-la-Jacques-Cartier. This region
has a Scandinavian spa, a riot of
winter attractions, and watersports
on Lac Saint-Joseph.

9 Grand Canyon des Chutes Sainte-Anne
MAP P3 ▪ Route 138 est,
Beaupré ▪ Adm

Only 30 minutes outside
the city is a series of waterfalls contained in a narrow
canyon. A breathtaking sight.

10 Chemin du Roy
MAP P3

The "King's Road"
(route 138) winds from
Montreal to Quebec.
Chemin du Roy is known
today by cyclists as the Route Verte
for its beautiful bike path that trails
alongside the St Lawrence River.

See map on pp92–3

Shopping and Markets

Strolling on Rue du Petit-Champlain

1 Rue du Petit-Champlain

A marvelous pedestrianized shopping concourse that features fashion boutiques, souvenir shops, restaurants, art galleries, theaters, and a park. Don't miss a ride on the Funiculaire.

2 Simons

MAP L4 ■ 20 côte de la Fabrique

Fashions for the whole family can be purchased here. Expect impeccable service from the staff.

3 Galeries de la Capitale

5401 Blvd des Galeries, off rte 310

One of the busiest shopping malls in the country with over 280 stores offering fashion, electronics, groceries, books, furniture, and more. A themed area for children includes a ferris wheel, roller coaster, and skating rink.

4 Quartier St-Roch

MAP J6

Along Rue St-Joseph and Boulevard Charest are a host of interesting boutiques, cafés, and microbreweries, as well as the famous Benjo toy store.

5 Place de la Cité

2600 Blvd Laurier, junction of hwys 175 and 720, Sainte-Foy

Southwest of town you will find shopper's heaven where three upscale malls converge. It has the largest concentration of exclusive boutiques in Quebec, and also a produce market and restaurants.

6 Le Grand Marché de Québec

This farmers' market is a cornucopia of the finest produce grown in the province (see p95).

7 J.A. Moisan

MAP J5 ■ 699 Rue St-Jean

Jean-Alfred's establishment began in 1871, making it the oldest grocery store in North America. Typical articles on sale at this charming store include fine condiments, meat, bread and pastries, and cheeses from around the world.

8 Les Promenades du Vieux-Québec

MAP L5 ■ 43 Rue de Buade

This tiny shopping cluster of unique boutiques also features the delightful Boutique de Noël, where you can buy unusual Christmas decorations throughout the year.

9 Marché Public de Sainte-Foy

920 Ave Roland-Beaudin, St-Foy ■ Rte 440

This public market is a mix between an age-old farmers' market and a contemporary grocery store. Being able to meet the grower face to face offers a satisfying assurance of the freshness of your purchases.

10 La Carotte Joyeuse

MAP J5 ■ 690 Rue St-Jean

Specialists in organically grown produce, this little grocery store sells baked goods as well as aromatic and medicinal herbs and spices.

Nightlife

1 Grand Théâtre de Québec

MAP H6 ■ 269 Blvd René-Lévesque Est

The Grand Théâtre de Québec showcases the talents of l'Orchestre Symphonique de Québec, Opéra de Québec, and an international line-up of musical stars (see p52).

2 Le Diamant

MAP K4 ■ 966 Rue St-Jean ■ (418) 692 5353 ■ www.lediamant.ca

A performing arts center across from Place d'Youville. The program here includes dance, music, drag, comedy, and more.

3 L'Inox

MAP J6 ■ 655 Grande Allée Est

This microbrewery in the city's Vieux-Port is a blessing for beer-lovers. The place has a clear passion for the stuff and offers a wide selection of homemade blondes, whites, ambers, reds, and browns.

4 Dagobert

MAP J6 ■ 600 Grande Allée Est

A large, popular three-storied club with live bands on the first floor, DJs upstairs, and regular theme nights and events. The action does not begin until after midnight.

5 La Korrigane

MAP J4 ■ 380 Rue Dorchester

Set in the St-Roch district, this friendly brewpub features a pretty terrace where locals can be seen sipping excellent craft beers. Enjoy the vibrant atmosphere and snack on organic meat and veggie burgers, prepared mainly from locally-sourced, seasonal produce.

6 Maelstrom Saint-Roch

MAP G5 ■ 181 Rue St-Vallier Est ■ (418) 523 0700

By day this is a coffee shop known for its healthy lunch menu and relaxed atmosphere. At night, how-ever, it turns into a vibrant cocktail bar. Try a coldbrew cocktail here.

7 Théâtre de la Bordée

MAP H4 ■ 315 Rue St-Joseph Est ■ (418) 694 9721 ■ www.bordee.qc.ca

Founded in 1976, this attractive theater stages a range of classical and contemporary performances from poetry to Shakespeare, with sets designed by luminaries such as Robert Lepage.

8 Théâtre Petit-Champlain

MAP M5 ■ 68 Rue du Petit-Champlain

This is one of the best small theaters in North America for design, ambiance, repertoire, and location. Entertaining perfor-mances of music, comedy, dance, and modern art.

Crowds at Palais Montcalm

9 Palais Montcalm

MAP L5 ■ 995 Place d'Youville

This multi-room theater offers performances from the biggest names in music, as well as a more intimate space for emerging artists.

10 Bar Ste-Angèle

MAP L5 ■ 26 Rue Ste-Angèle

Cozy and tucked-away live jazz and cocktail bar with a vintage vibe. It also has a good selection of local beers.

See map on pp92–3

Bars and Cafés

① Les Voûtes Napoleon
MAP J6 ▪ 680 Grande Allée Est

Local live music and a snug atmosphere, plus extremely friendly staff add to the ambiance of this brick-walled subterranean bar. They also offer a selection of local beers.

② Le Ninkasi du Faubourg
MAP J5 ▪ 801 Rue St-Jean

Named after the ancient Sumerian goddess of beer, this microbrewery also operates as a live music venue and has karaoke nights from Tuesdays to Sundays starting at 10pm.

③ Pub d'Orsay
MAP L5 ▪ 65 Rue de Buade

One of the city's most appealing pubs, both indoors and out, this is the perfect place to sample Quebec's famous microbrewery beers such as La Fin du Monde, Boréale, and Blanche de Chambly, and the unique taste of McKeown Cidre.

④ Bar Le Sacrilege
MAP J5 ▪ 447 Rue St-Jean

This pub with church pew seats has 14 different microbrews on tap, but that's not all it offers: it often doubles as a performance space for actors and musicians.

Outdoor tables at Bar Le Sacrilege

⑤ Cantook
MAP J5 ▪ 575 Rue St-Jean

Small but welcoming roaster and coffee shop offering a vast selection of excellent beans that you can purchase whole or enjoy on the premises.

⑥ Café Krieghoff
1091 Ave Cartier ▪ Bus No. 11

If you wish to venture into the heart of Quebec City's artistic community, there is no better place than a seat at this convivial café. Ideal for light meals and strong coffee, B&B accommodations are available too.

⑦ 1068 Wine and Cheese Bar
MAP L5 ▪ Le Château Frontenac, 1 Rue des Carrières

Named after the year of Quebec City's founding, this stylish wine bar in the famed Le Château Frontenac pours rich wines and offers one of the largest selections of Quebec cheeses in Canada.

⑧ L'Oncle Antoine
MAP M5 ▪ 29 Rue St-Pierre

One of the city's oldest surviving bars from 1754, L'Oncle Antoine is set in a stone cellar with a fireplace and an outdoor patio. Try the French onion soup with a refreshing pint of local beer.

⑨ La Barberie
MAP J4 ▪ 310 Rue St-Roch

Highlights of this eco-friendly brewery include a tasting room and a beer garden. There's no kitchen on-site but the staff will happily help you order in from restaurants nearby.

⑩ Chez Temporel
MAP L4 ▪ 25 Rue Couillard

On a quiet street, this popular meeting place has the best homemade croissants, *croque monsieurs* (baked ham and cheese sandwiches), and coffee in the province.

Restaurants

PRICE CATEGORIES
For a three-course meal for one with half
a bottle of wine (or equivalent meal),
taxes and extra charges.
....
$ under $40   **$$** $40–$80   **$$$** over $80

Elegant dining area at Café du Monde

① Café du Monde
MAP M5 ▪ 84 Rue Dalhousie
▪ (418) 692 4455 ▪ $$

In a lovely waterside location,
this Paris-style bistro serves
great food. Try the black pudding
with apple compote.

② Patente et Machin
MAP M4 ▪ 82 Rue St-Joseph
Ouest ▪ (581) 981 3999 ▪ $$

Casual, lively French restaurant
with the latest fresh offerings
written on a blackboard. Seafood
and meat dishes are prepared in
creative and surprising ways.

③ Restaurant Ophelia
MAP J6 ▪ 634 Grand
Allée Est ▪ (418) 524 8228 ▪ $$

Ophelia is a stylish restaurant
serving seafood, steak, and
braised Wagyu beef. The wine
list is good, but the cocktails
are even better.

④ Paillard
MAP K5 ▪ 1097 Rue St-Jean
▪ (418) 692 1221 ▪ $

Modern gourmet bakery and
café that's buzzing at brunch
and lunch time. Among the huge
variety of homemade delicacies,
the sweet and savoury croissants
are especially wonderful.

⑤ Le Champlain
MAP L5 ▪ 1 Rue des Carrières
▪ (418) 692 3861 ▪ $$$

Landmark classic French restaurant
that has been reinvented over the
years and serves regional cuisine.

⑥ Matto
MAP M4 ▪ 71 Rue St-Pierre
▪ (418) 266 9444 ▪ $$

Many of the pasta dishes at this
popular Italian restaurant are hand-
made by the owner's mother.

⑦ Restaurant Légende
MAP K4 ▪ 255 Rue St-Paul
▪ (418) 614 2555 ▪ $$$

Seasonal cuisine is taken to a high
art at this esteemed restaurant.

⑧ Bistro B
MAP H6 ▪ 1144 Ave Cartier
▪ (418) 614 5444 ▪ $$

Enjoy sophisticated modern dishes,
beautifully presented, at this cocktail
bar and bistro.

Snow outside Le Lapin Sauté

⑨ Le Lapin Sauté
MAP M5 ▪ 52 Rue du Petit-
Champlain ▪ (418) 692 5325 ▪ $$$

The French country fare at this
charming bistro includes rabbit-
centric dishes such as rabbit pie.

⑩ Le Saint-Amour
MAP K5 ▪ 48 Rue Ste-Ursule
▪ (418) 694 0667 ▪ $$$

The amazing menu at this fine-dining
spot includes wild boar, Canadian
sturgeon caviar, and local venison.

See map on pp92–3 ←

TOP 10 Excursions from Quebec City

Parc de la Chute-Montmorency

1 Parc de la Chute-Montmorency

MAP P3 ■ 2490 Ave Royale, Hwy 138 east

When the first settlers crossed the Atlantic and sailed up the St Lawrence River to this virgin area, they were greeted by the sight of these powerful waterfalls, which, at 272 ft (83 m), are higher than Niagara Falls. Take the cable car up and visit Manoir Montmorency (1781), with its interpretation center, boutiques, restaurant, and terrace with a view of the action. Other vantage points are also scattered about the park (see p34).

2 Île d'Orléans

This lovely island outside Quebec City is dotted with farms that produce many of the fruits, vegetables, and culinary specialties of the region. Designated a heritage site with over 600 preserved buildings, Île d'Orléans is a slice of history (see pp34–5).

3 Basilique Sainte-Anne-de-Beaupré

This huge cathedral site is always busy with religious pilgrims, who believe that the prayers of many others have been answered here (see pp32–3).

4 Mont Sainte-Anne

MAP P3 ■ 2000 Blvd Beau-Pré, Beaupré

A sensational outdoor playground 25 miles (40 km) east of Quebec City, the mountain is popular for world-class skiing, paragliding, mountain biking, or golfing at the 18-hole Le Grand Vallon course. With over 125 miles (200 km) of hiking trails, which double in the winter as paths for snowshoeing, dogsledding, and cross-country skiing, Mont Sainte-Anne defines the four-season personality of the province.

5 Grosse Île and Irish Memorial National Historic Site

MAP P3

This site commemorates the tragic events experienced by Irish immigrants who, escaping the potato famine in Ireland, were quarantined here only to die during the typhoid epidemic of 1847. Take the trolley to the village where you can admire historic buildings, and visit the 1847 Catholic chapel.

Snow geese gather on the plains at Cap Tourmente

6 Charlevoix
MAP P2

Nowhere is the spirit and passion of Quebec Province more obvious than in this 130-mile (200-km) coastal district of rolling hills, charming villages, and pastoral scenes. Baie St-Paul, with its heritage houses, is one of the most charming.

Hautes-Gorges-de-la-Rivière-Malbaie

7 Parc des Hautes-Gorges-de-la-Rivière-Malbaie
MAP P2 ■ Access via St-Aimé-des-Lacs on Rue Principale ■ Open daily ■ www.sepaq.com

This national park is one of Quebec's most stunning natural monuments. The steep slopes, beautiful natural surroundings, and the unusual course of the Malbaie River make this site unique. The point where the river valley takes a sharp 90-degree turn is a protected UNESCO area. Walk through the valley or, in the summer, join a guided cruise along the calm waters. You can also stay at the park overnight.

8 Cap Tourmente
MAP P3 ■ 570 Chemin du Cap-Tourmente

Drive 45 minutes east of Quebec City to see an incredible congregation of wild birds indigenous to the province. Over 180 species populate the area, the most photographed being the snow goose – thousands return to these fertile grounds every year.

9 Saguenay and Lac Saint-Jean
MAP Q1 ■ Parc national du Saguenay: 91 Notre-Dame, Rivière-Éternité

This fjord, leading inland to Lac Saint-Jean, is a designated protected area because it is frequented by beluga whales, dolphins, black bear, moose, and many other varieties of wildlife. Granite walls over 985-ft (300-m) high cast a mysterious and powerful aura over the maritime environment and give rise to the numerous fables and legends associated with the movement of its ocean tides.

10 Tadoussac
MAP Q1 ■ Boat trips: Croisières Dufour: 1-866 856 6668

Tadoussac's waterfront is backed by magnificent rocky cliffs and towering sand dunes, but the main attraction here lies offshore. Whale-watching boat trips take visitors out to view the minke, grey, and beluga whales in the Saguenay-St Lawrence Marine Park.

Streetsmart

**Hiker, Lac Saint-Jean,
Saguenay National Park**

Getting Around	**106**
Practical Information	**108**
Places to Stay	**112**
General Index	**118**
Acknowledgments	**124**
Phrase Book	**126**

Getting Around

Arriving by Air

Montreal's **Pierre Elliott Trudeau International Airport** is the main hub of the province, serviced by local, domestic, and international flights. From the airport, buses and taxis run to the city center.

Jean-Lesage International Airport is about 15 minutes drive from Quebec City. Several major US airlines, Air Canada, and Air Transat, a charter company with direct flights to Paris, all operate out of here.

Arriving by Train

VIA Rail is Canada's national passenger rail network. Safety and hygiene measures, timetables, ticket information, transport maps, and more can be obtained from the Via Rail website and individual stations. VIA Rail trains from other points in Canada, and **Amtrak** services from the US, pull in to Montreal's Gare Centrale. This is also where you connect to trains or buses for Quebec City and services to other Canadian cities.

Arriving by Sea

Cruise ships arriving in the Port of Montreal anchor at the Iberville Terminal, which is within walking distance of Vieux-Montréal. In Quebec City, meawhile, the cruise terminal is a short distance from Vieux-Port, the historic harbor.

Traveling by Car

To reach Montreal by car use either Hwy 401 from southern Ontario, which becomes Hwy 20 at the Quebec border, and cross the Pont Galipeau bridge, or take Hwy 40 from Ottawa, crossing the Pont Île aux Tourtres. The Cantons-de-l'Est autoroute (Hwy 10) is fed by US freeways 91 and 93, with other US East Coast travelers using Hwy 15.

Quebec City visitors can choose either Hwy 20 or Hwy 40 from Montreal, or Hwy 138 if traveling to Quebec City from the east.

Parking in both cities can be a challenge, with little street parking, short-lived meters, and overpriced parking lots. There's no denying, however, that having your own wheels makes exploring the wider province far easier. Both cities have offices for many of the major car rental companies, including Avis, Budget, and Alamo.

Traveling by Métro

The best way to travel around Montreal is by Métro, which is efficient, fast, and clean. The Métro operates Sun–Thu 5:30am–12:30am and Fri–Sat 5:30am–1am. The Métro fans out to all corners of the city; some of the major interconnecting stations are Berri-UQAM, Lionel-Groulx, Snowdon, and Jean-Talon. Quebec City has no Métro.

Traveling by Bus

Montreal's bus station (**Gare d'autocars de Montréal**) is at the intersection of three Métro lines in eastern downtown. There are two major bus stations serving Quebec City: **Gare du Palais**, under the railway station in the old town, and the **Sainte-Foy Terminal.**

Montreal's bus and Métro systems are both run by the **Société de Transport de Montréal** (the STM). Travel and hygiene information for both systems can be found on the STM website. Bus routes cover the entire city and some services run throughout the night, including the Express Bus 747 which runs between the airport and the city center every 30 minutes (every 7 minutes during rush hour). The journey takes around an hour and costs $10 one-way.

Quebec City Buses operate throughout the city. Note that both cities also have buses that serve the surrounding region, including **Transdev Limocar** to Cantons-de-l'Est and **Galland Buses** to Les Laurentides.

Traveling by Taxi

Taxis are plentiful in both cities' downtown areas, and are usually metered. Hail taxis from the street, or call a reputable taxi firm: **Taxi Diamond** in Montreal are reliable. Ride-hailing apps, such as Uber, also operate in the city.

Traveling on Foot

Both cities are supremely pedestrian-friendly. The "Underground City", Montreal's vast pedestrian network of tunnels and atriums, spans the entire city (and is great for days when the weather is less than perfect). There are also clearly marked walking trails – note that they share space with cyclists and sometimes in-line skaters.

Traveling by Bicycle

With over 400 miles (644 km) of bike paths around the city, Montreal is a very bike-friendly city. It is easy to hire a bike thanks to **Bixi**. The first public-bike system launched in North America, it offers over 6,200 self-service bikes at 540-plus stations across the city. A 24-hour pass lets you borrow bikes as often as you like during that period. Note Bixi is only available from April to November.

In Quebec City, the Champlain Promenade, Plains of Abraham, and the marina are particularly bike-friendly.

Traveling by Calèche

Calèches (horse-drawn carriages) ply many of Montreal and Quebec City's main streets. They are popular with tourists

but many are opposed to them, highlighting the number of horses injured in traffic each year.

Traveling by Boat

Since Montreal is an island city, it's possible to get around the city on the water. Shuttle boats (navettes) are in regular use, but only in fair weather, which fluctuates according to the winter ice pack. A shuttle service is available from the South Shore community of Longueuil (generally May until mid-October).

In Quebec City, **Traverse Québec-Lévis** runs ferry services across the Saint-Lawrence River to Lévis.

Both cities also offer a variety of boat tours (see p111).

Buying Tickets and Travel Cards

The same tickets are valid on both the Métro and buses in Montreal. A one-way fare on either Métro or bus is $3.50 (exact change needed on the bus); you can also get two trips for $6.50 or ten trips for $30. Tickets can also be used to transfer from Métro to bus; tickets are good for 2 hours from first use.

A good bet for visitors is the one-day pass for $10, or three consecutive days for $20.50.

Locals often use OPUS cards, with a reloadable smart chip. OPUS cards cost a one-time fee of $6, and can be recharged at all Métro stations via ticket machines or fare collectors.

Tickets for regional trains and buses can be purchased in person at the relevant train or bus stations. They can also be bought on the VIA Rail website or at the bus stations' websites.

DIRECTORY

ARRIVING BY AIR

Jean-Lesage International Airport
🌐 aeroportdequebec.com

Pierre Elliott Trudeau International Airport
🌐 admtl.com

ARRIVING BY TRAIN

Amtrak
🌐 amtrak.com

VIA Rail
🌐 viarail.ca

TRAVELING BY BUS

Galland Buses
🌐 galland-bus.com

Gare d'autocars de Montréal
🌐 gamtl.com

Gare du Palais
📞 (418) 525 3000

Quebec City Buses
🌐 rtcquebec.ca

Sainte-Foy Terminal
📞 (418) 650 0087

Société de Transport de Montréal
🌐 stm.info

Transdev Limocar
🌐 limocar.ca

TRAVELING BY TAXI

Taxi Diamond
🌐 taxidiamond.com

TRAVELING BY BICYCLE

Bixi
🌐 montreal.bixi.com

TRAVELING BY BOAT

Traverse
🌐 traversiers.com

Practical Information

Passports and Visas

For entry requirements, including visas, consult your nearest Canadian embassy or check the visa section of the **Canadian Government** website. Citizens of all US, EU, and British Commonwealth countries do not require visas, but must apply to enter in advance for an Electronic Travel Authorization (eTA) via the government website. All travelers must also enter the required information on the ArriveCAN app within 72 hours of their arrival in Canada.

Government Advice

Now more than ever, it is important to consult both your and the Canadian government's advice before traveling. The **UK Foreign and Commonwealth Office**, the **US Department of State**, the **Australian Department of Foreign Affairs and Trade**, and the **Government of Canada** offer the latest information on security, health, and local regulations.

Customs Information

You can find information on the laws relating to goods and currency taken in or out of Canada on the **Canada Border Services Agency** website.

Insurance

We recommend taking out a comprehensive insurance policy covering theft, loss of belongings, medical care, cancellations, and delays, and read the small print carefully. Canada does not have reciprocal health care agreements with other countries.

Health

Canada has a world-class healthcare system, and residents have access to free health care through provinces' and territories' health insurance plans. Canada does not, however, have reciprocal health agreements with other countries, so it is important to take out health insurance prior to visiting. You will be asked to present a valid credit card before receiving medical services.

Montreal and Quebec City are both well-equipped with top-notch hospitals, including **Centre Hospitalier Universitaire de Québec** and **Montreal General Hospital**. Montreal also has a large number of local community services centres (**CLSC**), which provide neighborhood residents with a range of medical and health-related services and tests.

For up-to-date information regarding COVID-19 vaccination requirements, consult government advice.

Smoking, Alcohol, and Drugs

Smoking is only permitted on outdoor patios. Recreational use of cannabis is legal in Canada, if you are 19 years of age or older. You are limited to carrying up to 30 grams of dried cannabis in public. While you can legally take cannabis from province to province, taking cannabis into another country can result in prosecution. Possession of illegal drugs may entail heavy fines and possibly jail time.

The legal limit for drivers in Canada is 80 mg of alcohol per 100 ml of blood or 0.08 per cent BAC (blood alcohol content). This is roughly equivalent to a small glass of wine or a pint of regular-strength beer.

ID

There is no requirement for visitors to carry ID, but you may be asked to present your passport to the police within 24 hours.

Personal Security

Montreal and Quebec City are relatively safe cities to visit, but petty crime like pickpocketing does take place in some areas. Use your common sense, keep valuables in a safe place, and be alert to your surroundings. If you have anything stolen, report the crime as soon as possible at the nearest police station. Get a copy of the crime report to claim on your insurance. Contact your embassy or consulate immediately if your passport is stolen or in the event of a serious crime or accident.

Info-Crime Montreal is a telephone and online

service for reporting crime, allowing witness anonymity. All municipal **police**, **ambulance** and **fire** stations in Quebec are connected via the 911 emergency system.

As a rule, Canadians are very accepting of all people, regardless of their race, gender or sexuality. In 2005, Canada became the fourth country in the world, and the first in the Americas, to legalize same-sex marriage. Montreal is home to one of the country's oldest, and biggest, LGBTQ+ populations. North America's first LGBTQ+ publication, *Les Mouches Fantastiques*, was founded here in 1918; the first Montreal Pride march took place in 1979 and, today, Montreal Pride (or Fierté Montréal) is one of the largest LGBTQ+ festivals in Canada. If you do feel unsafe, the **Safe Space Alliance** pinpoints your nearest place of refuge.

Indigenous peoples in Canada have faced historic prejudice and discrimination, with suffrage only being extended to Indigenous men and women in 1960. Today, a disproportionate number of Indigenous women go missing or are murdered each year. **Hope for Wellness** offers immediate mental health counselling and crisis intervention to Indigenous peoples across Canada.

Travelers with Specific Requirements

Both cities are well-equipped for travelers with specific require-ments. Most attractions, lodgings, and trans-portation agencies can accommodate your needs if you make them known at the time of booking. If you require further assistance, various local organizations, such as **Keroul** in Montreal, are a useful resource.The **CNIB Foundation** offers helpful information and advice for blind and partially sighted travelers.

Accessibility information for public transportation and travel are available from the **Canadian Transportation Agency**, which also provides an online guide for disabled visitors traveling by air. Montreal International Airport is equipped to assist travelers with particular requirements. Transportation from Quebec City airport can be arranged with **Transport Accessible du Québec**. The STM, Montreal's transportation authority, offers special vans for wheelchair users.

DIRECTORY

PASSPORTS AND VISAS

Canadian Government
W cic.gc.ca/english/visit/visas.asp

GOVERNMENT ADVICE

Australian Department of Foreign Affairs and Trade
W dfat.gov.au
W smartraveller.gov.au

Government of Canada
W canada.ca

UK Foreign and Commonwealth Office
W gov.uk/foreign-travel-advice

US State Department
W travel.state.gov

CUSTOMS INFORMATION

Canada Border Services Agency
W cbsa-asfc.gc.ca

HEALTH

Centre Hospitalier Universitaire de Québec
W chudequebec.ca

CLSC
W santemontreal.qc.ca

Montreal General Hospital
W muhc.ca

PERSONAL SECURITY

Emergencies
C 911

Hope for Wellness
W hopeforwellness.ca

Info-Crime Montreal
W infocrimemontreal.ca

Montreal Fire Department
C (514) 872 3800 (non-emergency)

Montreal Police Department
C (514) 280 2222 (non-emergency)

Safe Space Alliance
W safespacealliance.com

TRAVELERS WITH SPECIFIC REQUIREMENTS

Canadian Transportation Agency
W otc-cta.gc.ca

CNIB Foundation
W cnib.ca

Keroul (Montreal)
W keroul.qc.ca

Transport Accessible du Québec
W taq.qc.ca

Time Zone

Quebec is 5 hours behind Greenwich Mean Time (GMT) – the same time zone as New York City. At midday in Montreal, it will be 5pm in London, 9am in Los Angeles, and 3am in Sydney.

Money

Quebecers use the Canadian dollar ($). Most establishments accept major credit, debit, and prepaid currency cards. Contactless payments are widely accepted, however, it is always worth carrying some cash for smaller items, tickets, and tips. ATM machines are widely available. US currency is accepted in Canada, but you will get a better rate exchanging US dollars at a bank.

Waiters expect to be tipped 15 to 20 per cent of the total bill, hotel porters and housekeeping should be given $2–3 per bag or day, and taxi drivers appreciate 10 to 15 per cent of the fare.

Electrical Appliances

The whole of North America operates on a 110-volt, 60-cycle electrical system, with two- or three-pronged plugs. Equipment manufactured in other countries will need an adaptor.

Cell Phones and Wi-Fi

Most international mobile phones work across Quebec. To minimize fees, check with your local carrier about international calls, data plans, and roaming charges. US residents can upgrade their domestic cell phone plan to extend to Canada.

Pre-paid phone cards usually offer the best rates for international and long-distance dialing, and are sold in most drugstores and convenience stores.

Many restaurants, cafés, shops, and libraries provide free Wi-Fi, while many hotels offer it for free or at a minimal daily cost.

Post

Canada Post handles most postal services in Canada. Post offices and mailboxes are available across the province. Stamps can be bought from post offices, and some supermarkets, drug stores, and even corner grocery stores. Stamps cost from 92¢ for up to 30g within Canada, to $2.71 for up to 30g for international mail. Post office hours are generally 9am–6pm daily, and until 5pm on the weekends. Allow one to two weeks when sending mail overseas. Parcels may take upward of two weeks.

Weather

Early summer and fall are the best times to visit Quebec, when the climate is more temperate. If you are interested in the variety of winter sports on offer, plan your visit October to November or January to March.

Christmas is magical in both cities, but it is an extremely popular time to visit. Busier still are June and July, largely due to the region's packed festival calendar. Quebec City draws the crowds to its Carnaval each February.

The term "weather extremes" might have been invented in Quebec, where residents and visitors alike comment on variations from hour to hour. Temperatures range from 40º C (105º F) in summer to -40º C (-40º F) during winter. Packing rain gear is *de rigueur* and wearing layers of clothes that can be taken on and off is a sensible option.

Opening Hours

Shops in Quebec are generally open 8am–9pm on weekdays, and until 5pm on weekends. Montreal (and, to a certain extent, Quebec City) also has numerous 24-hour options, including grocery stores, supermarkets, and pharmacies. Banks and post offices generally open daily 9am–6pm, and until 5pm on weekends.

COVID-19 Increased rates of infection may result in temporary opening hours and/or closures. Always check ahead before visiting museums, attractions and hospitality venues.

Visitor Information

Quebec has a wealth of excellent and helpful tourist offices, offering maps, current event listings, and the like. For Montreal city, pop into the **Tourist Information Centre of Old Montreal**.

Centre Infotouriste de Montréal also has useful information on the city and province. In Quebec City, visit the well-stocked **Centre Infotouriste de Québec**.

The tourism office websites are equally packed with information, and are a superb source of practical information, travel tips, and city news.

If you are planning to visit a number of big-name sights, consider buying a discount card to save money. Montreal's **Passeport MTL** gives access to 23 attractions in a 72-hour period; the **Discovery Pass** offers unlimited admission for 12 months at over 80 National Parks that usually charge admission; and **City Passport** offer up to 50 per cent off entrance in seven major cities, including Montreal.

Trips and Tours

Montreal and Quebec City offer a wide variety of tours. Given the cities' pedestrian-friendly streets and sidewalks, walking tours are a decent option; among the top tours in Montreal are **Héritage Montréal** and **Kaleidoscope**. **Tours Voir Québec** in Quebec City offers walking and food tours, as well as day excursions to the Montmorency Falls.

The Vieux-Port is the major departure point for boat trips, including the **Amphi-bus**, a bus that morphs into a boat, and the glass-topped **Bateau-Mouche**; in Quebec City, hop aboard the **Croisières AML**.

Bus tours include the **Gray Line** Hop-On Hop-Off Double Decker Tour in Montreal, and the Gray Line Quebec City and Montmorency Falls Tour in Quebec City.

Language

While both English and French are the official languages of Canada, only French is officially used in the province of Quebec. Even so, most people speak English.

Taxes and Refunds

A Provincial Sales Tax (PST) and a nationwide, 5 per cent Goods and Services Tax (GST) apply to most goods and services in Quebec. There are also additional taxes on lodgings.

You may be eligible for a tax rebate under the Foreign Convention and Tour Incentive Program (FCTIP). Consult the **Revenue Agency** website.

Accommodation

A comprehensive list of accommodations can be found on the website of the **Quebec Tourist Board** and **Destination Canada**, Canada's official tourism site.

The Goods and Services Tax (GST) and Provincial Sales Tax (PST) must be paid on accommodations, as well as an additional accommodation tax (sometimes called Destination Marketing Fee). These taxes are usually paid on top of the advertised rates.

DIRECTORY

POST

Canada Post
w canadapost.ca

TOURIST OFFICES

Centre Infotouriste de Montréal
w mtl.org

Centre Infotouriste de Québec
w quebecregion.com

Visitor Information Centre of Old Montreal
w mtl.org

City Passport
w citypassports.com

Discovery Pass
w pc.gc.ca

Passeport MTL
w mtl.org

TRIPS AND TOURS

Amphi-bus
w montreal-amphibus-tour.com

Bateau-Mouche
w bateau-mouche.ca

Croisières AML
w croisieresaml.com

Gray Line
w grayline.com

Héritage Montréal
w heritagemontreal.org

Kaleidoscope
w tourskaleidoscope.com

Tours Voir Québec
w toursvoirquebec.com

TAXES AND REFUNDS

Revenue Agency
w canada.ca/en/revenue-agency

ACCOMMODATION

Destination Canada
w canada.trave

Quebec Tourist Board
w quebecregion.com

Places to Stay

PRICE CATEGORIES
For a standard, double room per night (with breakfast if included), taxes, and extra charges.

$ under $100 $$ $100–$200 $$$ over $200

Luxury Hotels

Hôtel Château Laurier, Quebec City

MAP J6 ▪ 1220 Place George-V Ouest ▪ (418) 522 8108 ▪ www.hotel chateaulaurier.com ▪ $$

This friendly hotel is in a nice spot facing Parc Georges-V and is within close proximity to the Parlement and the Parc des Champs-de-Bataille.

Fairmont Château Frontenac, Quebec City

MAP L5 ▪ 1 Rue des Carrières ▪ (418) 692 3861 ▪ www.fairmont. com/frontenac-quebec ▪ $$$

The Château Frontenac, in the center of Vieux-Québec, astounds guests with its beauty and luxury. It's decorated as a veritable museum of Canadiana, with a birch-bark canoe and stuffed polar bear in the lobby and artifacts on its walls (see p93).

Fairmont le Manoir Richelieu, La Malbaie

MAP Q2 ▪ 181 Rue Richelieu ▪ (418) 665 3703 ▪ www.fairmont.com/ richelieu-charlevoix ▪ $$$

This fabulous hotel, dating from 1929, offers a golf course, a casino, and an idyllic setting on the St Lawrence River. The hotel attracts US presidents, Hollywood stars, and high-rolling gamblers.

Fairmont Queen Elizabeth Hotel, Montreal

MAP H2 ▪ 900 Blvd René-Lévesque Ouest ▪ (514) 861 3511 ▪ www. fairmont.com/queen-elizabeth-montreal ▪ $$$

The royalty of Montreal hotels embodies grace and comfort. It is also well known as the location of John Lennon's famous "Bed-In" of 1969.

Fairmont Tremblant, Mont Tremblant

MAP N5 ▪ 3045 Chemin de la Chapelle ▪ (819) 681 7000 ▪ www.fairmont. com/tremblant ▪ $$$

Golf, spas, adventure activities, boutiques, and restaurants nestled in the heart of a village setting at the foot of a mountain.

Hôtel Birks, Montreal

MAP J1 ▪ 1240 Phillips Sq ▪ (514) 370 3000 ▪ www. hotelbirksmontreal.com ▪ $$$

This hotel is housed in the building Henry Birks once used as a storefront for his jewelery company. It is filled with intricate architectural details, and features a spa, French brasserie, and bar lounge.

Hôtel Bonaventure Montreal

MAP J2 ▪ 900 Rue de la Gauchetière Ouest ▪ (514) 878 2332 ▪ www.hotel bonaventure.com ▪ $$$

On top of the 17-story Place Bonaventure convention center, this hotel provides an oasis of comfort. The heated rooftop pool is surrounded by a lush garden.

Hôtel InterContinental, Montreal

MAP J2 ▪ 360 Rue St-Antoine Ouest ▪ (514) 987 9900 ▪ www. montreal.intercontinental. com ▪ $$$

The InterContinental connects with the Montreal World Trade Center via an atrium, where guests and visitors are offered a bonanza of shopping and leisure options under one roof.

Hôtel le Crystal, Montreal

MAP H2 ▪ 1100 Rue de la Montagne ▪ (514) 861 5550 ▪ www.hotelle crystal.com ▪ $$$

The dazzling chandelier, soaring windows, and leather seating in the lobby set the tone for this chic hotel, which offers stylish rooms and suites. Guests can use the well-equipped fitness center, which has its own indoor saltwater pool. The outdoor hot tub on the 12th floor gives great views of the city.

Le Germain, Montreal

MAP H2 ▪ 2050 Rue Mansfield ▪ (514) 849 2050 ▪ www.legermain hotels.com ▪ $$$

A former office building that has been beautifully transformed into a serene mid-century modern hotel in the midst of all the downtown activity. Le Germain is characterized by great food and impeccable service. The hotel's facade features a colorful mural by Michelle Hoogveld.

Ritz-Carlton Montreal

MAP H1 ■ 1228 Rue Sherbrooke Ouest ■ (514) 842 4212 ■ www.ritz montreal.com ■ $$$
A landmark of old-world charm and sophistication, this elegant Neo-Classical structure attracts an elite clientele often seen relaxing with cocktails or English tea in the courtyard garden. Book well in advance.

Historic Hotels and Manors

Auberge Bonaparte, Montreal

MAP K3 ■ 447 Rue St-François-Xavier ■ (514) 844 1448 ■ www.bona parte.com ■ $$
An elegant 19th-century boutique hotel in Vieux-Montréal, the Auberge Bonaparte has an excellent in-house French restaurant. Guests can enjoy complimentary breakfast on the lovely rooftop terrace.

La Marquise de Bassano, Quebec City

MAP L5 ■ 15 Rue des Grisons ■ (418) 692 0316 ■ www.marquise debassano.com ■ $$
This stylish B&B rises over a quiet street in Old Quebec. The 19th-century decor, stained glass, and high ceilings – even the original bells used to summon the servants – mark this as a legacy of Quebec's railroad history.

Manoir Maplewood, Waterloo

MAP Q6 ■ 26 Rue Clark, about 9 miles (14 km) north of Knowlton ■ (450) 920 1500 ■ www.manoir maplewood.com ■ $$
This exquisite inn was the mansion of Senator Asa Belknap Foster in 1864, who was a Canadian railroad tycoon. The restored building features ten elegant rooms with cream-colored linens and hardwood floors, plus a wine cellar in which tastings are held.

Auberge du Vieux-Port, Montreal

MAP K3 ■ 97 Rue de la Commune Est ■ (514) 876 0081 ■ www.lofts vieuxport.com ■ $$$
Soak up the atmosphere of Vieux-Montréal when staying at this beautifully restored hotel in a former warehouse on the riverfront. The lovely rooms reflect the building's history, with pine floors, wood beams, brass beds, and arched windows.

Auberge St-Antoine, Quebec City

MAP M4 ■ 8 Rue St-Antoine ■ (418) 692 2211 ■ www.saint antoine.com ■ $$$
This carefully restored warehouse offers one-of-a-kind decor, a waterfront setting, and amenities such as heated floors.

Château Versailles, Montreal

MAP A3 ■ 1659 Rue Sherbrooke Ouest ■ (514) 933 3611 ■ www.chateau versaillesmontreal.com ■ $$$
Myth and legend circulate when speaking about Château Versailles, partly because the four townhouses that it occupies were once home to Montreal's upper crust. Today the hotel welcomes a diverse guest list of performers, artists, and writers. A complimentary breakfast is included.

Épik, Montreal

MAP K3 ■ 171 Rue St-Paul Ouest ■ (514) 842 2634 ■ www.epik montreal.com ■ $$$
This beautifully restored 1723 building has been transformed into a sleek boutique hotel, but the history shines through, from the hardwood floors and original stone to the beamed ceilings. Plus, you can enjoy amenities like rain showers, fireplaces, and complimentary breakfast served in a skylit nook.

Le Saint-Sulpice, Montreal

MAP K3 ■ 414 Rue St-Sulpice ■ (514) 288 1000 ■ www.lesaint sulpice.com ■ $$$
Only steps from all the main attractions, this hotel, with its tranquil inner courtyard, is an oasis at the heart of the mayhem.

LHotel, Montreal

MAP K3 ■ 405 Rue St-Jacques ■ (514) 985 0019 ■ $$$
This boutique hotel and art gallery is housed in an 1870s French Revival building. The rooms are vibrant, contemporary, and eclectic in style, as is the restaurant, with its pop art and zebra-print chairs.

Manoir Hovey, North Hatley

MAP Q6 ▪ 575 Rue Hovey ▪ (819) 842 2421 ▪ www. manoirhovey.com ▪ $$$
This early 20th-century inn with white columns, palatial grounds, and antique-filled rooms, sits on the shores of Lake Massawippi. The Le Hatley restaurant has breathtaking views.

Boutique Hotels

ALT Hotel Griffintown, Montreal

MAP H2 ▪ 120 Rue Peel ▪ (844) 823 8120 ▪ www. althotels.com ▪ $$
This trendy hotel reflects the style of its hip neighborhood, with chic furnishings, recycled brick from the district's old buildings, and modern rooms with plump beds and cotton sheets.

Auberge Manoir le Tricorne, North Hatley

MAP Q6 ▪ 50 Rue Gosselin ▪ (819) 842 4522 ▪ www.manoirle tricorne.com ▪ $$
A charming hotel in a secluded location overlooking Lake Massawippi. Each room is different, but they are all cozy. Breakfast is included, and features eggs Benedict, casseroles, and quiche.

Le Pleasant, Sutton

MAP Q6 ▪ 1 Rue Pleasant, about 16 miles (25 km) south of Knowlton ▪ (450) 538 6188 ▪ www.le pleasant.com ▪ $$
Relax at this elegant boutique B&B, with dark-wood ceilings that are offset by snow-white sofas and colorful art. Le Pleasant capitalizes on its proximity to Mont Sutton with excellent ski deals.

Hôtel du Vieux-Quebec, Quebec City

MAP K4 ▪ 1190 Rue St-Jean ▪ (418) 800 7542 ▪ www.hvq.com ▪ $$$
Centrally located, modern hotel with a welcoming lounge area. Enjoy the complimentary walking tours plus breakfast baskets which are delivered to your room each morning.

Hôtel Gault, Montreal

MAP J3 ▪ 449 Rue Ste-Hélène ▪ (514) 904 1616 ▪ www.hotelgault.com ▪ $$$
The individually styled loft rooms, set in an 1871 warehouse, are a design-lover's dream, with Scandinavian fixtures and white-oak paneling, while the bathrooms have sleek freestanding tubs and heated floors.

Hôtel Nelligan, Montreal

MAP K3 ▪ 106 Rue St-Paul Ouest ▪ (514) 788 2040 ▪ www.hotel nelligan.com ▪ $$$
The Nelligan embraces the concept of boutique hotels, mixing contemporary furnishings with historic elements and designer decor. Features include a roof terrace, European cuisine, and a wine cellar, plus a shuttle bus to downtown.

Hôtel Place d'Armes, Montreal

MAP K2 ▪ 55 Rue St-Jacques ▪ (514) 842 1887 ▪ www.hotelplace darmes.com ▪ $$$
This captivating hotel represents the crowning glory of the Antonopoulos family of Quebec, who preserved much of Vieux-Montréal's heritage architecture. Throughout the hotel's refined rooms and suites, guests will experience old-world charm and comfort.

Hôtel St-Paul, Montreal

MAP J3 ▪ 355 Rue McGill ▪ (514) 380 2222 ▪ www. hotelstpaul.com ▪ $$$
The exterior of this Beaux Arts building is deceiving, for inside is minimalist comfort and savvy design. The Hambar cocktail bar is perfect for a late-night snack.

Hôtel Vogue, Montreal

MAP H1 ▪ 1425 Rue de la Montagne ▪ (514) 285 5555 ▪ www.hilton. com ▪ $$$
A large boutique hotel with a fine central location ideal for exploring all the sights and the nightlife of the city. It also has one of the city's finest restaurants, Le Société Bistro.

Le Germain Hôtel, Quebec City

MAP M4 ▪ 126 Rue St-Pierre ▪ (418) 692 2224 ▪ www.legermain hotels.com ▪ $$$
A mix of heritage details and contemporary design entice both business and leisure travelers here. In a great location surrounded by attractions, this tiny gem is a real find.

Le Petit Hôtel, Montreal

MAP K3 ▪ 168 Rue St-Paul Ouest ▪ (514) 940 0360 ▪ www.petithotel montreal.com ▪ $$$
Bright orange pops of

color play against old stone at this whimsical Vieux-Montréal hotel, housed in an elegant 19th-century building. Stylish rooms come in clothing sizes – S, M, L, XL – and the lobby café serves up potent espressos and silky red wines. Bicycles are also available for guests' use.

Mid-Range Hotels

Hôtel Château de l'Argoat, Montreal
MAP E3 ▪ 524 Rue Sherbrooke Est ▪ (514) 842 2046 ▪ www.hotel-chateau-argoat.com ▪ $$
Pleasant, good-value hotel in a lively neighborhood with eclectic decor. The decor in the rooms is eclectic, with a mix of modern and vintage furnishings. Room charges include breakfast and parking.

Hotel des Coutellier, Quebec City
MAP K4 ▪ 253 Rue St-Paul ▪ (418) 692 9696 ▪ www.hoteldescoutellier.com ▪ $$
Exposed brick, hardwood floors, and wonderful city views are offered from most rooms. Breakfast is delivered each morning by the amiable staff.

Hôtel Le Dauphin Centre-Ville, Montreal
MAP J3 ▪ 1025 Rue de Bleury ▪ (514) 788 3888 ▪ www.hotelsdauphin.ca ▪ $$
Good-value hotel featuring spacious modern rooms with hardwood floors, iMac desktop computers, Keurig coffee machines, and other such

extras. Fresh croissants are part of the complimentary breakfast.

Hôtel Manoir d'Auteuil, Quebec City
MAP K5 ▪ 49 Rue d'Auteuil ▪ (866) 662 6647 ▪ www.manoirdauteuil.com ▪ $$
This charming hotel, built in what used to be a private home, is located in the heart of the Old City. While the rooms and suites vary in size as well as decor, all are warm, welcoming, and equipped with modern amenities.

Hôtel Manoir Sherbrooke, Montreal
MAP D3 ▪ 157 Rue Sherbrooke Est ▪ (514) 845 0915 ▪ www.manoirsherbrooke.ca ▪ $$
A heritage exterior gives way to luxurious accommodations inside. Proud, friendly staff offer a 24-hour reception, suites with whirlpools, and a complimentary breakfast.

Hôtel Terrasse Dufferin, Quebec City
MAP L5 ▪ 6 Place de la Terrasse-Dufferin ▪ (418) 694 9472 ▪ www.terrassedufferin.net ▪ $$
Spectacular views of the Château Frontenac and St Lawrence River make for a memorable stay at this atmospheric hotel. The well-appointed rooms benefit from balconies and kitchenettes.

Hôtel Zero 1, Montreal
MAP M2 ▪ 1 Blvd René-Lévesque Est ▪ (514) 871 9696 ▪ www.zero1-mtl.com ▪ $$
This artsy urban hotel rises over the Quartier

des Spectacles, and offers stylish rooms and suites, all with kitchens, and spectacular views of the city skyline. The trendy roof terrace also provides a relaxing space from which to peruse the city below.

Le Château de Pierre, Quebec City
MAP L5 ▪ 17 Ave Ste-Geneviève ▪ (418) 694 0429 ▪ www.chateaudepierre.com ▪ $$
A million-dollar location attracts visitors to this charming hotel. Rooms are decorated in the style of the British colonial era and maintain an air of refinement. Rooms have views of the St Lawrence River or the garden.

Le Priori, Quebec City
MAP M4 ▪ 15 Rue Sault-au-Matelot ▪ (418) 692 3992 ▪ www.hotellepriori.com ▪ $$
This is an imaginative little hotel where down-filled duvets and slate showers complement wood-burning fireplaces and full kitchens.

Sofitel, Montreal
MAP B3 ▪ 1155 Rue Sherbrooke Ouest ▪ (514) 285 9000 ▪ www.sofitel-montreal.com ▪ $$
With access to galleries, museums, shopping, and nightlife, the Sofitel is a welcome mid-range chain addition to the city's supply of hotel rooms. Every frill and service is available, including excellent dining on-site at Le Renoir restaurant.

For a key to hotel price categories see p112

Auberges and B&Bs

Auberge aux Deux Lions, Quebec City
25 Blvd René-Lévesque Est ▪ (418) 780 8100 ▪ www.aubergeaux deuxlions.com ▪ $$
Close to all the major attractions, this B&B offers affordable but charming lodgings in a 20th-century building. There are also two family suites available.

Auberge des Gallant, Rigaud
MAP N6 ▪ 1171 Chemin St-Henri, Sainte-Marthe ▪ (450) 459 4241 ▪ www. aubergedesgallant.com ▪ $$
A year-round sanctuary, where deer roam the local landscape at dawn and dusk. The comfortable rooms include all modern amenities.

Auberge le Jardin d'Antoine, Montreal
MAP L1 ▪ 2024 Rue St-Denis ▪ (514) 843 4506 ▪ www.aubergele jardindantoine.com ▪ $$
This Quartier Latin hotel is located at a prime historic location and has friendly bilingual staff, modern accommodations, and a charming breakfast salon.

Auberge Les Bons Matins, Montreal
MAP C4 ▪ 1401 Rue Argyle ▪ (514) 931 9167 ▪ www.bonsmatins.com ▪ $$
Friendly service, freshly cooked gourmet breakfasts, and uniquely decorated rooms are features of this homey inn. Bright, original local art adorns the walls.

Auberge Lakeview Inn, Knowlton
MAP Q6 ▪ 50 Rue Victoria ▪ (450) 243 6183 ▪ www. aubergelakeviewinn.com ▪ $$
Set near Lac Brome, this antique-filled inn dates back to 1874. Room packages include breakfast and dinner. The inn houses a garden with a pool, where guests can lounge.

Auberge Ripplecove, Ayer's Cliff
MAP Q6 ▪ 700 Rue Ripplecove ▪ (819) 838 4296 ▪ www.ripplecove. com ▪ $$
Holders of the coveted Five-Star status from the Quebec Tourism authorities, this auberge garners praise from all corners for its romantic rooms, spectacular setting overlooking Lake Massawippi, and Four-Diamond dining.

Couette et Café le 253, Quebec City
MAP G4 ▪ 253 Rue de la Reine ▪ (418) 647 0590 ▪ www.le253.com ▪ $$
This is an LGBTQ+-friendly B&B in the St-Roch district. Choose from ensuite or shared bathrooms and enjoy full gourmet breakfasts on the lovely terrace.

Héritage Victorien B&B, Montreal
MAP L1 ▪ 305 Rue Ontario Est ▪ (514) 845 7932 ▪ www.montreal bedandbreakfast.ca ▪ $$
Housed in a restored Victorian mansion in the Quartier Latin area, this enchanting B&B is full of character. The beautiful rooms and suites feature period furniture and private bathrooms.

Hotel la Camarine, Beaupré
MAP P3 ▪ 10947 Blvd Ste-Anne ▪ (418) 827 5703 ▪ www.camarine.com ▪ $$
Situated at the foot of Mont-Ste-Anne's ski resort and hugging the banks of the Rivière Ste-Anne, Auberge La Camarine serves ample portions of pleasure and relaxation.

Hotel Verso, Magog
MAP Q6 ▪ 1150 Rue Principale Ouest, Magog ▪ (800) 567 2727 ▪ www. hotelverso.ca ▪ $$
On the shores of Lac Memphrémagog, this hotel has a mid-century modern vibe. The on-site Bistro Koz serves Mediterranean-style meals. The rooms are spacious with comfortable beds. There are some hiking trails, bike paths, waterways, wineries, and art galleries nearby.

L'Auberge Spa Watel, Ste-Agathe-des-Monts
MAP N5 ▪ 250 Rue St-Venant ▪ (819) 326 7016 ▪ www.hotels pawatel.com ▪ $$
A remarkable auberge with beautiful views of Lac des Sables. A range of equipment can be rented from the hotel, including fishing boats, kayaks, canoes, sail-boats, quad bikes, and snowmobiles.

Les Ancêtres, Île d'Orléans
MAP P3 ▪ 1101 Chemin Royal ▪ (418) 828 2718 ▪ $$
This auberge and restaurant is located in an ancestral home. Each room is named after the ancestors who once lived here. The on-site restaurant, once a favorite of

musician Félix Leclerc, is loved by locals and tourists alike.

Auberge Le Vincent, Quebec City

MAP H5 ▪ 295 St-Vallier Rue Est ▪ (581) 398 0653 ▪ www.hotelle vincent.com ▪ $$$
This charming red-brick hotel is located in the trendy Saint-Roch district. There are ten rooms with stylish, laid-back interiors. The innkeepers here are friendly, and breakfast is complimentary for guests.

Budget Hotels and Hostels

Auberge Alternative de Vieux-Montréal

MAP K3 ▪ 358 Rue St-Pierre ▪ (514) 282 8069 ▪ www.auberge-alternative.qc.ca ▪ No credit cards ▪ $
An independent, art-themed hostel in Vieux-Montréal with a choice of private or shared accom-modations. Bicycle and camping equipment is available for rent here, too.

Auberge de Jeunesse le P'tit Bonheur, Île d'Orléans

MAP P3 ▪ 186 côte Lafleur, St-Jean ▪ (418) 829 2588 ▪ www.leptit bonheur.com ▪ $
Enjoy dog-sledding and cross-country skiing while staying at this rustic auberge.

Auberge de la Paix, Quebec City

MAP L4 ▪ 31 Rue Couillard ▪ (418) 694 0735 ▪ www. aubergedelapaix.com ▪ $
This hip hostel has 60 beds with between two to eight travelers to a room. Breakfast is included.

Auberge Internationale de Québec, Quebec City

MAP K5 ▪ 19 Rue Ste-Ursule ▪ (418) 694 0755 ▪ www.auberge internationalede quebec.com ▪ $
Single, double or dorm choices are offered, with a fully equipped kitchen, games room, and yard.

Hotel Quartier des Spectacles, Montreal

MAP D3 ▪ 15 Rue Ste-Catherine Ouest ▪ (514) 849 2922 ▪ www.hotel quartierdesspectacles. com ▪ $
With hardwood floors and exposed red brick, this four-story building offers simple but spacious modern rooms. All rooms have a kitchenette and A/C, with a choice between shared and private bathrooms.

Le Gîte du Plateau Mont-Royal, Montreal

MAP D3 ▪ 185 Rue Sherbrooke Est ▪ (514) 284 1276 ▪ www.hostel montreal.com ▪ $
These clean and comfortable long-stay studios are located in the heart of Le Plateau, with access to Boulevard Saint-Laurent and Vieux-Montréal. The property also has an attached rooftop terrace.

Les Résidences Universitaires UQAM, Montreal

East Lodge: MAP M2 ▪ 303 Blvd René-Lévesque Est ▪ (514) 987 6669 ▪ West Lodge: MAP K2 ▪ 100 Rue St-Urbain ▪ (514) 987 7747 ▪ www.residences-uqam.qc.ca ▪ $
Clean and basic rooms and studios (some with

kitchenettes), as well as apartments, are available at these two Quartier Latin student residences. Guests have access to the fitness center. Open mid-May to mid-August.

Littoral, Quebec City

3710 Blvd Ste-Anne ▪ (418) 661 6901 ▪ www.littoralhotel spa.com ▪ $
Just a 10-minute drive outside of the city center, this heritage hotel has a modern feel to it. A 24-hour café, free park-ing, and spa are available. Rooms come equipped with a fridge, microwave, and coffee maker. Also on offer is the hotel's 4-star condo.

Montreal Y Hôtel & Auberge YWCA

MAP J2 ▪ 1355 Blvd René-Lévesque Ouest ▪ (514) 866 9941 ▪ www. ydesfemmesmtl.org ▪ $
This friendly, well-run, downtown YWCA has single, double, and triple rooms, which are simply furnished but also immac-ulate. Kitchen, laundry facilities, and Wi-Fi access are provided for guests' use.

HI Youth Hostel, Montreal

MAP G1 ▪ 1030 Rue Mackay ▪ (514) 843 3317 ▪ www.hostelling montreal.com ▪ $$
Rates vary at this Montreal hostelling institution, which has been in operation for more than 70 years. Located in the heart of downtown it offers affordable single rooms and dorms with up to ten beds.

For a key to hotel price categories see p112

General Index

Page numbers in **bold**
refer to main entries

99 Steps 14
1000 Islands 86

A

Accommodation 111–17
  budget tips 55
Air travel 106, 107
Amusement
  La Ronde Six Flags
    Amusement Park
    (Montreal) 50
  Parc Jean-Drapeau
    (Montreal) 47
André, Saint Brother
  (Alfred Bessette) 14, 15
Angélil, René 43
Anne de Beaupré, Sainte
  33
*Apelles Painting the Portrait
  of Campaspe* (Tiepolo) 24
Appalachian Mountains 87
Arbraska 51
Aréna Maurice-Richard
  (Montreal) 18
Art Mûr Gallery (Montreal)
  55
Auberge la Goéliche (Île
  d'Orleans) 34
Auberges 116–17
Avenue Duluth (Montreal)
  81
Avenue du Mont-Royal
  (Montreal) 81
Avenue du Parc (Montreal)
  81

B

B&Bs 116–17
Baillairgé, Thomas 33
Bank of Montreal Museum
  (Montreal) 64
Banks 110
Bars
  Downtown and Quartier
    Latin (Montreal) 73
  Mont-Royal to
    Hochelaga-Maisonneuve
    (Montreal) 82
  Quebec City 100
  Vieux-Montréal and Vieux
    Port (Montreal) 66
Basilique Notre-Dame
  (Montreal) 6, 7, 10,
  16–17, 44, 61
Basilique Sainte-Anne-de-
  Beaupré 7, 11, **32–3**, 102
Bellot, Dom Paul 14
Belvedere Kondiaronk
  (Montreal) 12, 81
Benedict XVI, Pope 14

Bessette, Alfred (Saint
  Brother André) 14, 15
Biking 49, 107
Biodôme (Montreal) 19,
  50–51
Biosphère (Montreal) 51,
  64
Birds
  Cap Tourmente 103
Black Star, The (Borduas)
  25
Boats
  boating 48
  cruise ships 106
  in Montreal 107
  Quebec City to Lévis
    Ferry 96
Boffrand, Germain 63
Bonet, Jordi 52
Borduas, Paul-Émile 42
  Black Star, The 25
Boulevard Saint-Laurent
  (Montreal) 12
Bourassa, Napoleon 71
Bourgeau, Victor 16, 17
Bourgeoys, Marguerite 62
Bouriché, Henri 16
Boutique hotels 114–15
Boutique Métiers d'Art du
  Québec (Quebec City)
  97
Brault, Father 15
Bridges of Montreal 86
Bromont 88
Brossard, Georges 19, 50
Budget travel 55
  hotels 117
Buses 106, 107

C

Cabaret du Capitole
  (Quebec City) 53
Cafés
  Mont-Royal to
    Hochelaga-Maisonneuve
    (Montreal) 82
  Quebec City 100
  Vieux-Montréal and Vieux
    Port (Montreal) 66
Calèches (horse-drawn
  carriages) 107
Callière, Louis-Hector 44
Camilien Houde lookout
  (Montreal) 12
Canada, creation of 40
Canadian Centre for
  Architecture 71
Canoeing 48
Cantons-de-l'Est 87
  attractions 88
  restaurants 89
Cap Tourmente 103
Carnaval de Québec 57

Carré St-Louis (Montreal)
  71
Cars
  driving 106
  motor racing 49, 56
Cartier, Sir George-Étienne
  Parc Montmorency
    (Montreal) 47
  Sir George-Étienne-
    Cartier National Historic
    Site (Montreal) 45, 63
Cartier, Jacques 40
  Île d'Orléans 34
  Parc du Mont-Royal
    (Montreal) 12
Casavant, Joseph 17
Cathedrals *see* Churches
Cemeteries
  Cimetière Mont-Royal
    (Montreal) 12
  Cimetière Notre-Dame-
    des-Neiges (Montreal)
    12
  Pointe-à-Callière
    (Montreal) 22
  Square Dorchester
    (Montreal) 47
Centaur Theatre (Montreal)
  53
Centre des Sciences de
  Montréal 50, 63, 64
Centre Sportif (Montreal)
  18
Champagne, Horace 35
Champaigne, Philippe de
  Tribute Money, The 25
Champlain, Samuel de 40
  La Citadelle (Quebec City)
    29
  Musée de la Civilisation
    de Québec (Quebec City)
    31
  Place Royale (Quebec
    City) 94
Chapelle du Sacré-Coeur
  (Montreal) 16
Chapelle Notre-Dame-de-
  Bon-Secours (Montreal)
  62
Chapelle Notre-Dame-de-
  Lourdes (Montreal) 71
Charlevoix 103
Charlier, Henri 14, 15
Château Frontenac
  (Quebec City) 8–9, 45,
  93, 95
Château Ramezay
  (Montreal) 44–5
Chemin du Roy 97
Children's attractions
  50–51
Chinatown (Montreal) 64,
  70–71

Chocolaterie de l'Île d'Orleans 35
Christian Brothers 21
Christmas 110
Churches and cathedrals
Basilique Notre-Dame (Montreal) 6, 7, 10, **16–17**, 44, 61
Basilique Sainte-Anne-de-Beaupré 7, 11, **32–3**, 102
Cathédrale Marie-Reine-du-Monde (Montreal) 69
Chapelle Notre-Dame-de-Bon-Secours (Montreal) 62
Chapelle Notre-Dame-de-Lourdes (Montreal) 71
Crypt Church (Montreal) 14
free concerts 54
Oratoire St-Joseph (Montreal) 12, **14–15**
St Patrick's Basilica (Montreal) 71
Cimetière Mont-Royal (Montreal) 12
Cimetière Notre-Dame-des-Neiges (Montreal) 12
Cirque du Soleil 43
Climate 110
Climbing 48
Clothes
budget tips 55
Coaticook, Gorge de 88, 90
Cohen, Leonard 43
Consulates 108
Cosmodôme (Laval) 51
COVID-19 110
Crime 108, 109
Croix du Parc du Mont-Royal (Montreal) 12, 81
Cruise ships 106
Crypt Church (Montreal) 14
Cultural Québécois 42–3
Currency 110
Customs and immigration 108, 109
Cycling 49, 107

D

Darling Foundry (Montreal) 63
Daudelin, Charles 17
Dauversière of La Flèche, Jerome le Royer, Sieur de la 62
Dawson, Sir William 70
De Gaulle, Charles 45
Deux-Montagnes 86
Dickens, Charles 62

Dion, Céline 17, 43
Disabled travelers 109
see also Travelers with specific needs
Dix, Otto
Portrait of the Lawyer Hugo Simons 24
Doctors 108
Domaine Steinbach (Île d'Orleans) 34
Downtown and Quartier Latin (Montreal) 68–75
bars and nightclubs 73
maps 68–9, 71
restaurants 74–5
shopping in Underground City 72
walk 71
Drapeau, Jean 19
Dreyfuss, Richard 43
Dubois Berthelot de Beaucours, Josué 44
Dufresne, Oscar and Marius 19
Duplessis, Maurice 41
Durham, Lord 40
Durnford, Lt-Colonel Elias Walker 28, 44

E

Electrical appliances 110
Emergency services 109
Entertainment
budget tips 55
performing arts venues 52–3
Éperon Building (Montreal) 22
Events 56–7
Excursions
from Montreal 84–91
from Quebec City 102–3

F

Faubourg Saint-Jean-Baptiste (Quebec City) 95
Ferry, Quebec City to Lévis 96
Festivals 54, 56–7
Festival d'Été de Québec 57
Festival International de Jazz de Montréal 56
Festival Montréal en Lumière 57
Tam-Tam Festival (Montreal) 13
Fêtes de la Nouvelle-France 57
Rendez-vous ès TRAD 57
Tam-Tam Festival (Montreal) 13
Fire services 109
Fireworks 56

First Nations 40
First Nations Garden (Montreal) 20
McCord Museum (Montreal) 69
Missisquoi Bay 90
Food and drink
budget tips 55
local and Québécois cuisine 91
see also Restaurants
Football 49
Fortifications
La Citadelle (Quebec City) 8–9, 11, **28–9**, 44, 93
Fortin, Marie-Thérèse 52
François I, King of France 40
Free events 54–5
Frelighsburg 88
French nationalism 70
Front de Libération du Québec (FLQ) 41
Fuller, Buckminster 51
Fur trade 62

G

Galerie d'art Inuit Brousseau (Quebec City) 97
Galleries see Museums and galleries
Gardens see Parks and gardens
Gay Village (Montreal) 71
George IV, King of England 70
Gothic Revival architecture 16
Grand Canyon des Chutes Sainte-Anne 97
Grand Prix du Canada 56
Grand Théâtre de Québec (Quebec City) 52
Grosse Île 102
Guardo, Joseph 14

H

Hanganu, Dan S. 22
Health care 108, 109
Hiraoka, Hisato 16
Historic hotels and manors 113–14
Historic sites 44–5
History 40–41
Hochelaga-Maisonneuve (Montreal) see Mont-Royal to Hochelaga-Maisonneuve
Horatio Walker Studio (Île d'Orleans) 35
Horses
calèches (horse-drawn carriages) 107
riding 49
Hospitals 108, 109
Hostels 117

Hôtel de Ville (Montreal) 45, 61
Hôtel du Parlement (Quebec City) 96
Hotels 111–17
Houde, Camillien 21
Hudson 85

I
Ice hockey 49
Île de Bacchus 34
Île d'Orléans 7, 11, **34–5**, 102
Insectarium (Montreal) 19, 50
Insurance 108
Internet 110
Indigenous experiences 41
Inuit peoples
    Galerie d'art Inuit Brousseau (Quebec City) 97
Irish Memorial National Historic Site 102

J
Jardin Botanique (Montreal) 6, 19, **20–21**, 26–7
Jardins des Gouverneurs (Quebec City) 95
Jazz 56
Johannsen, Herman "Jackrabbit" 37
John XXIII Pavilion 14
Joseph the Boarder (Quebec City) 30
Judith with the Head of Holopherne, Didon (Mantegna) 24
Just for Laughs Festival 56

K
Keroack, Lucien 21
Knowlton 88
Kondiaronk Lookout (Montreal) 12, 81

L
L'Abbaye de Saint-Benoît-du-Lac 88
Lac aux Castors (Montreal) 13, 81
Lac Brome 90
Lac de Rêve (Montreal) 20, 26–7
Lachine Rapids 46
La Citadelle (Quebec City) 7, 8–9, 11, **28–9**, 44, 93
Lac Massawippi 90
Lac Mégantic 90
Lac Memphrémagog 88
Lac Saint-Jean 103, 104–5
La Forge-à-Pique-Assaut (Île d'Orléans) 35
Laliberté, Alfred 47

Lamb, Thomas W. 53
Lanaudière 86
Language, phrase book 126–7
La Ronde Six Flags Amusement Park (Montreal) 50
Laser Quest (Montreal) 51
Laurentians *see* Les Laurentides
Laurier, Sir Wilfrid 47
Laviolette, Sieur de 86
Le Capitole de Québec (Quebec City) 53
Le Chemin des Vignobles de l'Estrie 88
Leclerc, Félix 35, 42, 46
Leduc, Ozias
    Mauve Twilight 25
Le Grand Marché de Québec (Quebec City) 95
Le Gros Bourdon (Montreal) 16
Leonardo da Vinci 33
Lepage, Robert 53
Le Plateau Mont-Royal (Montreal) 79
Les Amis de la Montagne (Montreal) 13
Les FrancoFolies de Montréal 56
Les Glissades de la Terrasse-Dufferin (Quebec City) 97
Les Laurentides 11, **36–7**, 85
Les Petits Chanteurs du Mont-Royal (Montreal) 15 Levasseur, René Nicholas 90
Le Théâtre de L'Oeil (Montreal) 51
Le Vignoble Ste-Pétronille (Île d'Orléans) 35
Liberal Party 41
Libraries
    Jardin Botanique (Montreal) 21
L'Îlot des Palais 96
L'International des Feux Loto-Québec (Montreal) 56
Little Italy (Montreal) 81
Luxury hotels 112–13

M
McCord Museum (Montreal) 69
McGill, James 70
McGill University (Montreal) 55, 70
Maison de la Littérature (Quebec City) 96
Maison Smith (Montreal) 13, 81

Maisonneuve, Paul de Chomedey, Sieur de 23, 62
    Croix du Parc du Mont-Royal (Montreal) 12
Maisons de la Culture 54, 80
Manoir Mauvide-Genest (Île d'Orléans) 35
Mantegna, Andrea
    Judith with the Head of Holopherne, Didon 24
Maps
    Île d'Orléans 35
    Les Laurentides 37
    Montreal 6
    Montreal: Downtown and Quartier Latin 68–9, 71
    Montreal: excursions 84–5, 87
    Montreal: Mont-Royal to Hochelaga-Maisonneuve 78, 81
    Montreal: Parc du Mont-Royal 13
    Montreal: Parc Olympique 19
    Montreal: Vieux-Montréal and Vieux Port 60–61, 63
    Montreal and Quebec City highlights 10–11
    Quebec City 7, 92–3, 95
    Quebec City: excursions 102
Marathon, Montreal 49
Marché Bonsecours (Montreal) 38–9, 44, 62, 63
Marché Jean-Talon (Montreal) 80
Marché Maisonneuve (Montreal) 18
Marie-Victorin, Brother 21
Markets
    Montreal 18, 80
    Quebec City 95, 98
Martineau, Aline 94
Masson, Raymond 55
Maurault, Olivier 17
Mauve Twilight (Leduc) 25
Métro (Montreal) 106, 107
Missisquoi Bay 90
Mobile phones 110
Money 110
Mont Owl's Head 90
Mont-Rolland 36
Mont-Royal to Hochelaga-Maisonneuve (Montreal) 78–83
    bars and cafés 82
    maps 78, 81
    restaurants 83
    walk 81
Mont Sainte-Anne 102

Mont Sutton 90
Mont Tremblant 37
Mont Tremblant Village 58–9, 85
Montcalm, General 45, 95
Montérégie 86
Montgomery, General Richard 63
Montmorency Falls 7, 34
Montreal
 Basilique Notre-Dame **16–17**
 children's attractions 50
 Downtown and Quartier Latin 68–75
 excursions 84–91
 festivals and events 56–7
 historic sites 44–5
 history 40–41
 hotels 112–17
 Jardin Botanique (Montreal) **20–21**
 map 6
 Mont-Royal to Hochelaga-Maisonneuve 78–83
 Montreal for free 54–5
 Musée des Beaux-Arts de Montréal **24–5**
 Oratoire St-Joseph **14–15**
 Parc du Mont-Royal **12–13**
 Parc Olympique **18–19**
 performing arts venues 52–3
 Pointe-à-Callière **22–3**
 spectator sports 49
 travel 106–7
 Vieux-Montréal and Vieux Port 60–67
Morrice, James Wilson
 Venice, Looking out over the Lagoon 24
Motor racing 49, 56
Mountain climbing 48
MTL Zipline (Montreal) 49, 64
Museums and galleries
 free days 54
 Bank of Montreal Museum (Montreal) 64
 Biosphère (Montreal) 51, 64
 Boutique Métiers d'Art du Québec (Quebec City) 97
 Canadian Centre for Architecture 71
 Centre des Sciences de Montréal 50, 63, 64
 Château Ramezay (Montreal) 44–5
 La Citadelle (Quebec City) 28
 Cosmodôme (Laval) 51

Museums and galleries (cont.)
 Darling Foundry (Montreal) 63
 Galerie d'art Inuit Brousseau (Quebec City) 97
 Insectarium (Montreal) 19, 50
 McCord Museum (Montreal) 69
 Maison Smith (Montreal) 81
 Morrin Centre, Quebec City 96
 Musée de l'Amérique Francophone (Quebec City) 30
 Musée d'Art Contemporain de Montréal 70
 Musée des Beaux-Arts de Montréal 6, 7, 11, **24–5**, 54, 69
 Musée Château Dufresne (Montreal) 19
 Musée Château Ramezay (Montreal) 62–3
 Musée de la Civilisation de Québec (Quebec City) 7, 11, **30–31**, 93
 Musée du Fort (Quebec City) 97
 Musée Marguerite-Bourgeoys (Montreal) 62
 Musée National des Beaux-Arts du Québec (Quebec City) 96
 Musée de l'Oratoire (Montreal) 14
 Musée Redpath (Montreal) 55, 70
 Pointe-à-Callière (Montreal) 6, 7, 10, **22–3**, 61
 Pôle Culturel du Monastère des Ursulines (Québec) 96
 Séminaire de Québec (Quebec City) 30
 "Univers Maurice-Richard" (Montreal) 18
Music
 festivals 56–7
 performing arts venues 52
 Les Petits Chanteurs du Mont-Royal (Montreal) 15

N
National Historic Sites
 Irish Memorial 102
 Pointe-à-Callière (Montreal) **22–3**
 Sir George-Étienne-Cartier (Montreal) 45, 63

National parks
 Parc des Hautes-Gorges-de-la-Rivière-Malbaie 103
 Parc National du Canada de la Mauricie 87
 Parc National de la Jacques-Cartier 97
 Parc National du Mont-Mégantic 90
 Parc National du Mont-Orford 88
 Parc National du Mont-Tremblant 37
 Saguenay National Park 103, 104–5
Nationalism, French 70
Nelligan, Émile 42
Neo-Classical architecture 14
Newton, Irene 24
Nightclubs
 Downtown and Quartier Latin (Montreal) 73
 Quebec City 99
Notebaert, Gérard 14

O
Observatoire de la Capitole (Quebec City) 94
October Crisis (1970) 41
Octobre (Tissot) 24
O'Donnell, James 16, 17
Old Customs House (Montreal) 64
Olmsted, Frederick Law 12, 13
Olympic Games, Montreal (1976) 18
Opening hours 110
Oratoire St-Joseph (Montreal) 12, **14–15**
Orchards, the 90
Ostell, John 23
Outaouais 85
Outdoor activities 48–9
Outremont (Montreal) 80

P
Paintings, trompe-l'oeil 94
Papineau, Louis-Joseph 71
Parc de la Chute-Montmorency 102
Parc de la Gorge de Coaticook 88, 90
Parc des Hautes-Gorges-de-la-Rivière-Malbaie 103
Parc Linéaire Le P'tit Train du Nord 48, 87
Parc National du Canada de la Mauricie 87

Parc National de la
  Jacques-Cartier 97
Parc National du Mont-
  Mégantic 90
Parc National du Mont-
  Orford 88
Parc National du Mont-
  Tremblant 37
Parent, Lucien 14
Parks and gardens 46–7, 54
  Jardin Botanique
    (Montreal) 6, 19, **20–21**,
    26–7
  Parc de l'Artillerie,
    Quebec City 97
  Parc Cavalier du Moulin
    (Quebec City) 47
  Parc des Champs-de-
    Bataille (Quebec City) 45,
    47, 94
  Parc de la Francophonie
    (Quebec City) 47
  Parc Jean-Drapeau
    (Montreal) 46–7, 61
  Parc Lafontaine
    (Montreal) 46, 81
  Parc Maisonneuve
    (Montreal) 46
  Parc du Mont-Royal
    (Montreal) 6, 7, 10,
    12–13, 46, 79
  Parc Montmorency
    (Quebec City) 47
  Parc Olympique
    (Montreal) 6, 10, **18–19**,
    79
Parti Québécois (PQ) 41
Passports 108, 109
Performing arts venues
  52–3
Perrault, Henri-Maurice 61
Personal security 108–109
Peterson, Oscar 42–3
Pharmacies 108
Phrase book 126–7
Place des Arts (Montreal) 52
Place du Canada
  (Montreal) 47
Place de la Dauversière
  (Montreal) 62
Place de l'Hôtel de Ville
  (Quebec City) 95
Place Gare Viger 64
Place Jacques-Cartier
  (Montreal) 45, 62
Place Royale (Montreal)
  44
Place Royale (Quebec City)
  31, 94
Place D'Ypuville 96
Plage de l'Horloge 64
Plains of Abraham, Battle
  of the (1759) 45, 47, 95
Planétarium Rio Tinto
  Alcan (Montreal) 18, 51
Pôle-des-Rapides 46

Police 108, 109
Police Stables (Montreal)
  13
Porte Saint-Louis (Quebec
  City) 96
*Portrait of the Lawyer Hugo
  Simons* (Dix) 24
Portrait of a Young Woman
  (Rembrandt) 24
Postal services 110
Price, Bruce 93
Prus, Victor 52

Q

Quai de l'Horloge
  (Montreal) 63, 64
Quartier Latin (Montreal)
  see Downtown and
  Quartier Latin
Quartier Petit-Champlain
  (Quebec City) 94, 95
Quebec City 92–101
  bars and cafés 100
  cultural Québécois 42–3
  excursions 102–3
  festivals and events 57
  further attractions 97
  historic sites 44–5
  history 40–41
  hotels 116–17
  La Citadelle **28–9**
  local and Québécois
    cuisine 42
  maps 7, 92–3, 95
  Musée de la Civilisation
    de Québec **30–31**
  nightlife 99
  performing arts venues
    52–3
  Quebec City for free
    54–5
  restaurants 101
  Separatism 31
  shopping and markets
    98
  spectator sports 49
  The best of the rest 96
  travel 106–7
Quebec City to Lévis Ferry
  96

R

Rafting 48
Railways 106, 107
Ramezay , Claude de 62
Rappelling 48
Referendum (1995) 41
Rembrandt
  *Portrait of a Young
    Woman* 24
Rénard, Jules 19
Restaurants
  budget tips 55
  Cantons-de-l'Est 89
  Downtown and Quartier
    Latin (Montreal) 74–5

Restaurants (cont.)
  Mont-Royal to
    Hochelaga-Maisonneuve
    (Montreal) 83
  Quebec City 101
  Vieux-Montréal and
    Vieux Port (Montreal)
    67
  see also Food and drink
Richard, Maurice 18
Richler, Mordecai 43
Rigaud 85
Riopelle, Jean-Paul 36, 42
  Wheel, The 25
Robitaille, Luc 53
Roman Catholic Church
  41
Route Saint-Armand
  90
Roy, Gabrielle 42
Royal 22nd Regiment
  29
Rue Saint-Denis
  (Montreal) 80–81

S

Safdie, Moshe 30, 93
Safety 108, 109
Saguenay National Park
  103, 104–5
Ste-Adèle 36
Ste-Agathe-des-Monts
  37
St-Jovite 37
St Lawrence River 6,
  40
St Patrick's Basilica
  (Montreal) 71
St-Sauveur-des-Monts
  36
Séminaire de Québec
  (Quebec City) 30
Séminaire St-Sulpice
  (Montreal) 17, 61
Separatism 31
Sherbrooke 88
Shopping
  opening hours 110
  Quebec City 98
  Underground City
    (Montreal) 72
  Vieux-Montréal and
    Vieux Port (Montreal)
    65
Simons, Hugo 24
Sir George-Étienne-
  Cartier National
  Historic Site
  (Montreal) 45, 63
Skating 48
Skiing 48–9
Smith, Hosea B. 13
Snowmobiling 49
Snowshoeing 48
Soccer 49
Spectator sports 49

Sports 48–9
Square Dorchester (Montreal) 47
Square Victoria (Montreal) 64
Stade Olympique (Montreal) 18, 76–7
Station Touristique Duchesnay 97
Sulpician Order 61, 86
Swimming 48

T

Tadoussac 103
Taillibert, Roger 18
Tam-Tam Festival (Montreal) 13
Tango Libre (Montreal) 54
Taxis 106–7
Telephones 110
Tennis 49
Terrasse-Dufferin (Quebec City) 95
Terrasse Pierre-Dugua-de-Mons (Quebec City) 97
Teuscher, Henry 19, 21
Théâtre d'Aujourd'hui (Montreal) 52
Théâtre de la Bordée (Quebec City) 53
Théâtre du Nouveau Monde (Montreal) 52
Théâtre du Petit Champlain Maison de la Chanson (Quebec City) 53
Théâtre de Quat'Sous (Montreal) 52
Théâtre du Rideau Vert (Montreal) 52
Théâtre de Verdure (Montreal) 55
Tickets, for travel 107
Tiepolo, Giovanni Battista
Apelles Painting the Portrait of Campaspe 24
Time zone 110
Tipping 110
Tissot, James
Octobre 24
Toboggans
Les Glissades de la Terrasse-Dufferin (Quebec City) 97
Tour Montréal (Montreal) 18, 76–7
Tourist offices 110, 111
Tours and trips 111
Trains 106, 107
Travel 106–7
budget tips 55

Travel cards 107
Travel insurance 108
Travel safety advice 108, 109
Travelers' checks 110
Travelers with specific needs 109
Travers, Mary 42
Tribute Money, The (Champaigne) 25
Trips and tours 111
Trois-Rivières 86–7
Trompe-l'oeil paintings 94

U

Underground City (Montreal) 72
Underground railway (Montreal) 106, 107
UNESCO 103
Union Act (1841) 40
University, McGill (Montreal) 55, 70

V

Val-David 37, 87
Val-Morin 36
Van Dyck, Anthony 94
Van Horne, Cornelius 45
Venice, Looking out over the Lagoon (Morrice) 24
Venne, Alphonse 14
Viau, Dalbé 14
Victoria, Queen of England 64
Vieux-Montréal and Vieux Port (Montreal) 6, 60–67
bars and cafés 66
maps 60–61, 63
restaurants 67
shopping 65
The best of the rest 64
walk 63
Vieux Port (Montreal)
see Vieux-Montréal and Vieux Port
Ville d'Estérel 36
Villiers, Roger 15
Visas 108, 109

W

Walker, Horatio 35
Walks 107
Downtown and Quartier Latin (Montreal) 71
Mont-Royal to Hochelaga-Maisonneuve (Montreal) 81
Vieux-Montréal and Vieux Port (Montreal) 63
walking tours 55

Waterfalls
Montmorency Falls 7, 34
Parc de la Chute-Montmorency 102
Waterways 46–7
Weather 110
Whales
Tadoussac 103
Wheel, The (Riopelle) 25
Wildlife
Cap Tourmente 103
Lac Saint-Jean 103
Tadoussac 103
Wolfe, General James 40, 45, 95

Y

Youth hostels 55
Youville Pumping Station Interpretation Center (Montreal) 23

Z

Zipline, MTL (Montreal) 49, 64
Zoos
Biodôme (Montreal) 19, 50–51
Insectarium (Montreal) 19, 50
Zoo de Granby 88

Acknowledgments

Author

Gregory B. Gallagher is a freelance writer, editor, photographer, musician and historian based in his native Montreal. He writes travel articles for the National Geographic Society, *Smithsonian Magazine*, Virgin Airlines, The Globe and Mail's *Dreamscapes Magazine*, Royal Canadian Geographic Society, and more.

Additional contributor
Annelise Sorensen

Publishing Director Georgina Dee

Publisher Vivien Antwi

Design Director Phil Ormerod

Editorial Michelle Crane, Rachel Fox, Freddie Marriage, Scarlett O'Hara, Sally Schafer, Jackie Staddon

Cover Design Maxine Pedliham, Bess Daly

Design Tessa Bindloss, Marisa Renzullo

Picture Research Susie Peachey, Ellen Root, Lucy Sienkowska, Oran Tarjan

Cartography Subhashree Bharti, Tom Coulson, Martin Darlison, Suresh Kumar, James Macdonald, Casper Morris

DTP Jason Little, George Nimmo

Production Nancy-Jane Maun

Factchecker Taraneh Ghajar Jerven

Proofreader Susanne Hillen

Indexer Hilary Bird

Illustrator chrisorr.com

First edition created by Sargasso Media Ltd, London

Revisions team Avanika, Hansa Babra, Parnika Bagla, Subhashree Bharati, Rebecca Flynn, Aishwarya Gosain, Sumita Khatwani, Taiyaba Khatoon, Shikha Kulkarni, Jordan Lambley, Alison McGill, Pamela MacNaughtan, Halima Mohammed, Chhavi Nagpal, Anjasi Nongkynrih Nyshadham, Kanika Praharaj, Vagisha Pushp, Anuroop Sanwalia, Mark Silas, Beverly Smart, Sarah Snelling, Avantika Sukhia, Hollie Teague, Priyanka Thakur, Stuti Tiwari, Vinita Venugopal, Tanveer Abbas Zaidi

Commissioned Photography Demetrio Carrasco, Alan Keohane, Rough Guides/Tim Draper

Picture Credits

Alamy Stock Photo: Rubens Abboud 20tl, 57cb; Adwo 18bc; All Canada Photos 96cb; All Canada Photos/Pierre Philippe Brunet 86cra; Tibor Bognar 11cl; Marc Bruxelle 56bl; Canada 95cra; canadabrian 37tl; Chad Case 48tl; Ian G Dagnall 12cl, 80bl; Danita Delimont/Walter Bibikow 36cl, /Cindy Miller Hopkins 55cl, /Rob Tilley 17tl, / Jamie & Judy Wild 35crb; dbimages/dbtravel 12br, 55br; Songquan Deng 34br; Design Pics Inc/Destinations/David Chapman 88cra, /First Light/Yves Marcoux 103clb; Vlad Ghiea 85t; Jorge Garrido 66crb; Hemis/Jean-Pierre Degas 48br, /Philippe Renault 7tr, 13cr, 43t, 91cra, 97cb; imageBROKER/Christian GUY 97cra, /David Chapman 15tr; Ken Gillespie Photography 3tl, 58–9; Terrance Klassen 11bl; Lebrecht Music and Arts Photo Library 40cb; Priyanka Madia 94br; Megapress 49cl, 75cra; Nikreates 4cra; Organica 21b; Mehul Patel 16–17; RGB Ventures/Superstock/Robert Huberman 11cra; Rolf Hicker Photography 4b, 44t; VWPics/ Hal Beral 17c; Tracey Whitefoot 21tr; Xinhua 54tl.

Bridgeman Images: AGIP 42tl.

Cafe du Monde: 101tl.

Centre des Sciences de Montréal: ShootStudio /Jean-Francois Lemire 50bl.

La Champagnerie: David Afriat 66cla.

Corbis: All Canada Photos/Perry Mastrovito 2tr, 38–9; AWL/Alan Copson 47br; Bettman 41clb; First Light/Philippe Henry 87clb; Hemis/Philippe Renault 101crb; Louis Hennepin 40t; Icon SMI/ Minos Panagiotakis 49tr.

La Distillerie Montréal: Jessika Duquette 73tr.

Dreamstime.com: Bonnyblue 64tr; Michel Bussieres 4cl, 31br, 46b, 79t; Mircea Costina 84cra; Danechka 61crb; Martial Genest 2tl, 8–9, 51cra; Vlad Ghiea 62t; Christian De Grandmaison 20bl; Howiewu 86bl; Wangkun Jia 10cl, 11crb, 28cl, 28br, 32clb, 32–3, 61tl, 69br, 93tl; Chon Kit Leong 33br; Meunierd 10b, 12–13, 18–19, 96tr; Mikeaubry 6clb; Martine Oger 81clb; Peanutroaster 28–9; Denis Pepin 11br, 37br; Photal 16clb; Pictureguy66 103tr; Isabel Poulin 53br; Sandra Richardson 29crb; Manon Ringuette 64clb; Louise Rivard 46tr; Scottbeard 102tl; Think Design Manage 76–7; Jannis Werner 10cla.

Espace pour la Vie Montréal: Jardin Botanique de Montréal/Michel Tremblay 20cr; Planetarium Rio Tinto Alcan/Sebastien Gauthier 4t, / Jean-François Hamelin 18crb.

Les Fêtes de la Nouvelle-France: Simon Armstrong 57tr.

Getty Images: AFP/Rogerio Barbosa 14tr, 15clb; C Flanigan 99clb; Posnov / Moment 1.

Holder Restaurant-Bar: 67tr.

Le Capitole: 53t.

Le Cercle: Dylan Page 100bl.

Lesters Deli: 83bl.

Manoir Mauvide-Genest: 35tl.

Mont Sutton: Isabel Nehera 90b.

The Montréal Museum of Fine Arts: Photo Denis Farley 11tr, 54b; Adaline Van Horne Bequest, Photo Christine Guest, Giovanni Battista Tiepolo *Apelles Painting the Portrait of Campaspe* (c.1726); Oil on canvas; 57.4 x 73.7 cm (1945.929) 24ca; Mrs. R. MacD. Paterson Bequest, Rembrandt Harmensz. van Rijn *Portrait of a Young Woman (Magdalena van Loo?* (c.1668); Oil on canvas; 56.3 x 48 cm (1949. 1006) 24crb; Gift of Lord Strathcona and family,

Photo Brian Merrett, James Tissot *October* (1877) Oil on canvas; 216 x 108.7 cm (1927.410) 24bl; Purchase; Dr. and Mrs. Max Stern Bequest, Photo Brian Merrett, Philippe de Champaigne *The Tribute Money* (c.1663–5) Oil on canvas; 138.5 x 188 cm (1999.1) 25tl.

Musée d'art contemporain de Montréal: John Londono 70b.

Musée de la civilisation de Québec: Jessy Bernier 30br, 31tl; Nicola-Frank Vachon 30–31.

Noël Eternel: 65br.

Parks Canada: Mathieu Dupuis 47cl; Miguel Legault 63clb.

Pointe-à-Callière: 23cb; Caroline Bergeron 22–3; SMQ/Studio du Ruisseau 22bl, /Michel Julien 22crb.

Quartier Petit Champlain: Llamaryon/Marion Desjardins 92tl.

Redpath Museum, McGill University: Torsten Bernhards 68cla, 70tr.

Rex by Shutterstock: Canadian Press 43clb; Design Pics 4cla; Fotos International 42br.

Ritz-Carlton Montréal: Maison Boulud/ Alexandre Parent 74b.

Robert Harding Picture Library: Tibor Bognár 93br; imageBROKER/David Chapman 45crb; Nikhilesh Haval 14bl; Yves Marcoux 98tl; Perry Mastrovito 79crb.

Royal Bromont: Le Cellier du Roi par Jérôme Ferrer/Rodolf Noel 89cr.

Shutterstock.com: Kristi Blokhin 4clb, meunierd 19bl, Alina Reynbakh 41tr.

SuperStock: age fotostock/Terrance Klassen 36–7; All Canada Photos/Robert Chiasson 34–5.

Théâtre du Nouveau Monde: Yves Renaud 52tl.

Théâtre du Rideau Vert: Jean-Francois Hamelin 52crb.

Tourisme Montréal: 26–7, 80l; Matthias Berthet 73bl; Canadian Tourism Commission 56t, /Alice Gao 82cla; Marc Cramer 71crb; La Ronde (Member of the Six Flags Family) 50t; Le Centre Eaton de Montréal/ Stéphan Poulin 72cra; Montréal Museum of Fine Arts 69tl; Musée Marguerite-Bourgeoys et Chapelle Notre-Dame-de-Bon-Secours 60cla.

Tourisme Saguanay-Lac-Saint-Jean: Jean Tanguay 3tr, 104–5.

Ville Montréal: Daniel Choiniere 51bl.

Cover

Front and spine: **Getty Images:** Posnov / Moment.

Back: **Alamy Stock Photo:** Dellnesco crb; **AWL Images:** Alan Copson tl; **Dreamstime. com:** Aladin66 cl, Photogolfer tr; **Getty Images:** Posnov / Moment b.

Pull Out Map Cover

Getty Images: Posnov / Moment.

All other images © Dorling Kindersley

For further information see: www.dkimages.com

Penguin
Random
House

First edition 2004

Published in Great Britain by
Dorling Kindersley Limited
DK, One Embassy Gardens, 8 Viaduct
Gardens, London SW11 7BW, UK

The authorised representative in the EEA is
Dorling Kindersley Verlag GmbH. Arnulfstr.
124, 80636 Munich, Germany

Published in the United States by
DK Publishing, 1745 Broadway, 20th Floor,
New York NY 10019, USA

Copyright © 2004, 2022 Dorling
Kindersley Limited
A Penguin Random House Company

22 23 24 25 10 9 8 7 6 5 4 3 2 1

A CIP catalog record is available
from the British Library.

A catalog record for this book is available
from the Library of Congress.

ISSN 1479-344X

ISBN 978-0-2414-7225-5

Printed and bound in China

www.dk.com

*As a guide to abbreviations in visitor information
blocks:* **Adm** = *admission charge;* **D** = *dinner;*
L = *lunch.*

MIX
Paper from
responsible sources
FSC™ C018179

This book was made with Forest
Stewardship Council ™ certified
paper – one small step in DK's
commitment to a sustainable future.
For more information go to
www.dk.com/our-green-pledge

Phrase Book

In Emergency

Help!	Au secours!	oh sekoor
Stop!	Arrêtez!	aret-ay
Call a doctor!	Appelez un médecin!	apuh-lay uñ medsañ
Call an ambulance!	Appelez une ambulance!	apuh-lay oon oñboo-loñs
Call the police!	Appelez la police!	apuh-lay lah poh-lees
Call the fire department!	Appelez les pompiers!	apuh-lay leh poñ-peeyay

Communication Essentials

Yes/No	Oui/ Non	wee/noñ
Please	S'il vous plaît	seel voo play
Thank you	Merci	mer-see
Excuse me	Excusez-moi	exkoo-zay mwah
Hello	Bonjour	boñzhoor
Goodbye	Au revoir	oh ruh-vwar
Good night	Bonsoir	boñ-swar
What?	Quel, quelle?	kel, kel
When?	Quand?	koñ
Why?	Pourquoi?	poor-kwah
Where?	Où?	oo

Useful Phrases

How are you?	Comment allez-vous?	kom-moñ talay voo
Very well	Très bien	treh byañ
Pleased to meet you.	Enchanté de faire votre connaissance.	oñshoñ-tay duh fehr votr kon-ay-soñs
Where is/are…?	Où est/sont…?	oo ay/soñ
Which way to…?	Quelle est la direction pour…?	kel ay lah deer-ek-syoñ poor
Do you speak English?	Parlez-vous anglais?	par-lay voo oñg-lay
I don't understand.	Je ne comprends pas.	zhuh nuh kom-proñ pah
I'm sorry.	Excusez-moi.	exkoo-zay mwah

Useful Words

big	grand	groñ
small	petit	puh-tee
hot	chaud	show
cold	froid	frwah
good	bon	boñ
bad	mauvais	moh-veh
open	ouvert	oo-ver
closed	fermé	fer-meh
left	gauche	gohsh
right	droite	drwaht
straight ahead	tout droit	too drwah
entrance	l'entrée	l'on-tray
exit	la sortie	sor-tee

Shopping

How much does this cost?	C'est combien s'il vous plaît?	say kom-byañ seel voo play
I would like…	je voudrais…	zhuh voo-dray
Do you have?	Est-ce que vous avez?	es-kuh voo zavay
What time do you open?	A quelle heure vous êtes ouvert?	ah kel urr voo zet oo-ver
What time do you close?	A quelle heure vous êtes fermé?	ah kel urr voo zet fer-may
This one.	Celui-ci.	suhl-wee-see
That one.	Celui-là.	suhl-wee-lah
expensive	cher	shehr

Do you take credit cards?	Est-ce que vous acceptez les cartes de crédit?	es-kuh voo zaksept-ay leh kart duh krehdee
cheap	pas cher, bon marché	pah shehr, boñ mar-shay
size, clothes	la taille	tye
size, shoes	la pointure	pwañ-tur
white	blanc	bloñ
black	noir	nwahr
red	rouge	roozh
yellow	jaune	zhohwn
green	vert	vehr
blue	bleu	bluh

Types of Shop

antique store	le magasin d'antiquités	maga-zañ d'oñteekee-tay
bakery	la boulangerie	booloñ-zhuree
bank	la banque	boñk
bookstore	la librairie	lee-brehree
cake shop	la pâtisserie	patee-sree
cheese shop	la fromagerie	fromazh-ree
chemist	la pharmacie	farmah-see
convenience	le dépanneur	deh-pan-urrstore
department store	le grand magasin	groñ maga-zañ
delicatessen	la charcuterie	sharkoot-ree
gift shop	le magasin de cadeaux	maga-zañ duh kadoh
fruit and vegetable store	le marchand de légumes	mar-shoñ duh lay-goom
grocery store	l'alimentation	alee-moñta-syoñ
market	le marché	marsh-ay
newsstand	le magasin de journaux	maga-zañ duh zhoor-no
post office	la poste, le bureau de poste	pohst, booroh duh pohst
supermarket	le supermarché	soo pehr-marshay
smoke shop	la tabacie	tabah-see
travel agent	l'agence de voyages	l'azhoñs duh vwayazh

Sightseeing

abbey	l'abbaye	l'abay-ee
art gallery	la galerie d'art	galer-ree dart
bus station	la gare d'autobus	gahr door-to-boos
cathedral	la cathédrale	katay-dral
church	l'église	l'aygleez
garden	le jardin	zhar-dañ
library	la bibliothèque	beebleeo-tek
museum	le musée	moo-zay
train station	la gare	gahr
tourist information office	le bureau d'information	booroh duh infor-mah-syoñ
town hall	l'hôtel de ville	l'ohtel duh veel

Staying in a Hotel

Do you have a vacant room?	Est-ce que vous avez une chambre?	es-kuh voo-zavay oon shambr
double room, with double bed	la chambre pour deux personnes, avec un grand lit	shambr poor duh pehr-son avek un groñn lee
twin room	la chambre à deux lits	shambr ah duh lee

single room | la chambre pour une personne | shambr poor oon pehr-son
room with a bath, shower | la chambre avec salle de bains, une douche | shambr avek sal duh bañ, oon doosh
I have a reservation. | J'ai fait une réservation. | zhay fay oon rayzehrva-syoñ

Eating Out

Have you got a table?	Avez-vous une table de libre?	avay-voo oon tahbl duh leebr
I want to reserve a table.	Je voudrais réserver une table.	zhuh voo-dray rayzehr-vay oon tahbl
The bill please.	L'addition s'il vous plaît.	l'adee-syoñ seel voo play
Waitress/ waiter	Madame, Mademoiselle/ Monsieur	mah-dam, mah-demwahzel/ muh-syuh
menu	le menu, la carte	men-oo, kart
fixed-price menu	le table d'hôte	tahb-luh dote
cover charge	le couvert	koo-vehr
wine list	la carte des vins	kart-deh vañ
glass	le verre	vehr
bottle	la bouteille	boo-tay
knife	le couteau	koo-toh
fork	la fourchette	for-shet
spoon	la cuillère	kwee-yehr
breakfast	le petit déjeuner	puh-tee deh-zhuh-nay
lunch	le déjeuner	deh-zhuh-nay
dinner	le dîner	dee-nay
main course	le plat principal	plah prañsee-pal
appetizer, first course	l'entrée, le hors d'oeuvre	l'oñ-tray, or-duhvr
dish of the day	le plat du jour	plah doo zhoor
wine bar	le bar à vin	bar ah vañ
café	le café	ka-fay

Menu Decoder

baked	cuit au four	kweet oh foor
beef	le boeuf	buhf
beer	la bière	bee-yehr
boiled	bouilli	boo-yee
bread	le pain	pan
butter	le beurre	burr
cake	le gâteau	gah-toh
cheese	le fromage	from-azh
chicken	le poulet	poo-lay
chips	les frites	freet
chocolate	le chocolat	shoko-lah
coffee	le café	kah-fay
dessert	le dessert	deh-ser
egg	l'oeuf	l'uf
fish	le poisson	pwah-ssoñ
fresh fruit	les fruits frais	frwee freh
garlic	l'ail	l'eye
grilled	grillé	gree-yay
ham	le jambon	zhoñ-boñ
ice cream	la crème glacée	crem glas-ay
ice cubes	les glaçons	glas-oñ
lamb	l'agneau	l'anyoh
lemon	le citron	see-troñ
meat	la viande	vee-yand
milk	le lait	leh
mineral water	l'eau minérale	l'oh meeney-ral
oil	l'huile	l'weel
onions	les oignons	leh zonyoñ

fresh orange juice	jus d'orange frais	zhu d'oroñzh fray
fresh lemon juice	jus de citron frais	zhu de see-troñ fray
pepper	le poivre	pwavr
pork	le porc	por
potatoes	pommes de terre	pom-duh tehr
rice	le riz	ree
roast	rôti	row-tee
salt	le sel	sel
sausage, fresh	la saucisse	sohsees
seafood	les fruits de mer	frwee duh mer
snails	les escargots	leh zes-kar-goh
soup	la soupe, le potage	soop, poh-tazh
steak	le bifteck	beef-tek, stek
sugar	le sucre	sookr
tea	le thé	tay
vegetables	les légumes	lay-goom
vinegar	le vinaigre	veenaygr
water	l'eau	l'oh
red wine	le vin rouge	vañ roozh
white wine	le vin blanc	vañ bloñ

Numbers

0	zéro	zeh-roh
1	un, une	uñ, oon
2	deux	duh
3	trois	trwah
4	quatre	katr
5	cinq	sañk
6	six	sees
7	sept	set
8	huit	weet
9	neuf	nerf
10	dix	dees
11	onze	oñz
12	douze	dooz
13	treize	trehz
14	quatorze	katorz
15	quinze	kañz
16	seize	sehz
17	dix-sept	dees-set
18	dix-huit	dees-weet
19	dix-neuf	dees-nerf
20	vingt	vañ
30	trente	tront
40	quarante	karoñt
50	cinquante	sañkoñt
60	soixante	swasoñt
70	soixante-dix	swasoñt-dees
80	quatre-vingts	katr-vañ
90	quatre-vingt-dix	katr-vañ-dees
100	cent	soñ
1,000	mille	meel

Time

one minute	une minute	oon mee-noot
one hour	une heure	oon urr
half an hour	une demi-heure	urr duh-me urr
one day	un jour	urr zhorr
Monday	lundi	luñ-dee
Tuesday	mardi	mar-dee
Wednesday	mercredi	mehrkruh-dee
Thursday	jeudi	zhuh-dee
Friday	vendredi	voñdruh-dee
Saturday	samedi	sam-dee
Sunday	dimanche	dee-moñsh

Montreal and Quebec Selected Street Index

Montreal

Amherst, Rue	M1
Barre, Rue	G3
Beaudry, Rue	M1
Belmont, Rue	J2
Berri, Rue	L1
Bishop, Rue	G1
Bleury, Rue de	K2
Bonsecours, Rue	L3
Camillien-Houde, Voie	C2
Canada, Place du	H2
Cathcart, Rue	J2
Cathédrale, Rue de la	H2
Champ-de-Mars, Rue du	L2
Champlain, Rue	F3
Commune, Rue de la	K3
Côte-des-Neiges, Chemin de la	B2
Côte-Ste-Catherine, Chemin de la	C1
Crescent, Rue	G2
Dalhousie, Rue	H3
Dauversière, Place de la	L3
Dorchester, Square	H2
Drummond, Rue	H1
Duluth Est, Avenue	E2
Eleanor, Rue	H3
Émery, Rue	L1
Fortifications, Ruelle des	K2
Gauchetière Est, Rue de la	M2
Gauchetière Ouest, Rue de la	K2
Guy, Rue	G2
Henri-Julien, Avenue	E2
Hôtel-de-Ville, Avenue de l'	L2
Jacques-Cartier, Place	L3
Jeanne-Mance, Rue	K2
Laurier Est, Avenue	E1
Laval, Avenue	D2
Le Royer, Cours	K3
Longueuil, Rue de	J3
Mackay, Rue	G1
Maisonneuve Est, Boulevard de	M1
Maisonneuve Ouest, Boulevard de	J1
Mansfield, Rue	H1
Marie-Anne Est, Rue	E2

Mayor, Rue	J1
McGill College, Avenue	J1
McGill, Rue	J3
Metcalfe, Rue	H1
Montagne, Rue de la	H2
Montcalm, Rue de	M1
Montigny, Rue de	K1
Mont-Royal Est, Avenue du	E2
Mont-Royal Ouest, Avenue du	D2
Mont-Royal, Boulevard	D2
Moyne, Rue le	J3
Normand, Rue	J3
Notre-Dame Est, Rue	M2
Notre-Dame Ouest, Rue	J3
Ontario Est, Rue	L1
Papineau, Avenue	F3
Parc-Lafontaine, Avenue du	E2
Parc, Avenue du	D2
Peel, Rue	H2
Pins Ouest, Avenue des	D3
Place Royale	K3
Place Victor-Hugo	G3
Prince Arthur Est, Rue	D3
Prince, Rue	J3
Queen-Mary, Chemin	A1
Rachel Est, Rue	E2
René-Lévesque Est, Boulevard	M2
René-Lévesque Ouest, Boulevard	J2
Robin, Rue	M1
Roy Est, Rue	E2
St-Alexandre, Rue	J2
St-André, Rue	M1
St-Antoine Est, Rue	M2
St-Antoine Ouest, Rue	J2
St-Denis, Rue	L2
St-Dominique, Rue	K1
Ste-Catherine Est, Rue	M1
Ste-Catherine Ouest, Rue	J1
Ste-Elisabeth, Rue	L2
St-François-Xavier, Rue	K3

St-Henri, Rue	J3
St-Hubert, Rue	M1
St-Jacques, Rue	J3
St-Jean, Rue	K3
St-Joseph Est, Boulevard	E1
St-Joseph Ouest, Boulevard	D1
St-Laurent, Boulevard	K2
St-Louis, Rue	L2
St-Louis, Square	L2
St-Mathieu, Rue	G1
St-Norbert, Rue	K1
St-Paul Est, Rue	L3
St-Paul Ouest, Rue	K3
St-Pierre, Rue	K3
St-Sulpice, Rue	K3
St-Timothée, Rue	M1
St-Urbain, Rue	K2
St-Vincent, Rue	L3
Sanguinet, Rue	L2
Sherbrooke Est, Rue	E3
Sherbrooke Ouest, Rue	J1
Stanley, Rue	H1
Union, Avenue	J1
University, Rue	J2
Versailles, Rue	G2
Victoria, Square	J2
Viger Est, Avenue	L2
Viger Ouest, Avenue	J2
Visitation, Rue de la	M1
Wellington, Rue	J3
William, Rue	J3
Wolfe, Rue	M1
Youville, Place d'	K3

Quebec City

Abraham, Côte d'	J5
Arago Est, Rue	H5
Armes, Place d'	L5
Auteuil, Rue d'	K5
Buade, Rue	L5
Carrières, Rue des	L5
Champlain, Boulevard	L6
Charest Est, Boulevard	J4
Charlevoix, Rue	L4
Chevrotière, Rue de la	J6
Citadelle, Côte de la	K6
Couillard, Rue	L4
Couronne, Rue de la	H4
Dalhousie, Rue	M5
Dauphine, Rue	K5

Dorchester, Rue	H4
Dufferin-Montmorency, Avenue	K5
Dufferin, Terrasse	L5
Fabrique, Côte de la	L4
Fleurie, Rue	J4
Gare-du-Palais, Rue de la	K4
Garneau, Rue	L4
George-VI, Avenue	K6
George-V, Place	K6
Grande Allée Est	J6
Jardins, Rue des	L5
Mont-Carmel, Rue	L5
Palais, Côte du	K4
Parlementaires, Rue des	K6
Petit-Champlain, Rue du	M5
Place Royale	M5
Porte, Rue de la	L5
Prévost, Rue	J5
Remparts, Rue des	L4
René-Lévesque, Boulevard	J6
Richelieu, Rue	J5
Roi, Rue du	J4
Salaberry, Avenue de	G6
Sault-au-Matelot, Rue	M4
Sous-le-Fort, Rue	M5
St-André, Rue	L4
St-Antoine, Rue	M4
St-Augustin, Rue	L5
St-Denis, Avenue	L5
Ste-Anne, Rue	K5
Ste-Claire, Rue	H5
Ste-Famille, Rue	L4
Ste-Geneviève, Avenue	L5
Ste-Geneviève, Côte	J5
Ste-Ursule, Rue	K5
St-Flavien, Rue	L4
St-Gabriel, Rue	J5
St-Jean, Rue	J5
St-Joachim, Rue	J5
St-Louis, Rue	L5
St-Paul, Rue	K4
St-Pierre, Rue	M4
St-Vallier Est, Rue	K4
Tourelle, Rue de la	J5
Trésor, Rue du	L5
Université, Rue de l'	L4
Youville, Place d'	K5
Youville, Rue d'	K5